CULTURES OF THE WORLD®

JORDAN

Coleman South

 Marshall Cavendish
Benchmark
New York

PICTURE CREDITS
Cover photo: © Lindsay Hebberd / CORBIS
A.S.A.P. Ltd: 12, 16, 37, 40, 42, 64, 119 • alt.TYPE / Reuters: 43, 44, 46, 56, 59, 67, 70, 71, 81, 89, 91, 100, 102, 112, 120, 123
• Audrius Tomonis: 135 • Bes Stock: 38, 39 • Björn Klingwall: 11, 101, 106, 113, 116 • Chris Barton, Middle East Pictures:
7, 19, 23, 108 • Focus Team, Italy: 10, 51, 73, 74, 97, 107 • HBL Network Photo Agency: 58, 63, 75 • Hulton Deutsch: 27,
30, 35 • Hutchison / Eye Ubiquitous: 69, 110, 111, 121, 131 • Jamie Simson: 22, 99 • Lonely Planet Images: 1, 3, 4, 6, 9, 15,
18, 57, 60, 72, 94, 109, 114, 115, 117 • MCIA—Thomas Khoo: 130 • Photolibrary: 5, 45, 80, 84, 85, 90, 98, 118, 122, 124, 129
• Reuters: 65, 79 • Susanna Burton: 50, 76 • Tropix: 52, 53, 55

PRECEDING PAGE
Children merrily playing in the fertile fields of the Jordan Valley.

Publisher (U.S.): Michelle Bisson
Editors: Deborah Grahame, Mabelle Yeo, Johann Abang Kassim
Copyreader: Daphne Hougham
Designer: Bernard Go Kwang Meng
Cover picture researcher: Connie Gardner
Picture researchers: Thomas Khoo, Joshua Ang

Marshall Cavendish Benchmark
99 White Plains Road
Tarrytown, NY 10591
Web site: www.marshallcavendish.us

© Times Editions Private Limited 1997
© Marshall Cavendish International (Asia) Private Limited 2008
All rights reserved. First edition 1997. Second edition 2008.
® "Cultures of the World" is a registered trademark of Times Publishing Limited.

Originated and designed by Times Editions Private Limited
An imprint of Marshall Cavendish International (Asia) Private Limited
A member of Times Publishing Limited

Library of Congress Cataloging-in-Publication Data
South, Coleman, 1948–
    Jordan / Coleman South. — 2nd ed.
        p. cm. — (Cultures of the world)
    Summary: "Provides comprehensive information on the geography, history, wildlife, governmental structure, economy, cultural
        diversity, peoples, religion, and culture of Jordan"—Provided by publisher.
    Includes bibliographical references and index.
        ISBN 978-0-7614-2080-4
    1. Jordan—Juvenile literature. I. Title. II. Series.
    DS153.S57 2007
    956.95—dc22   2006101726

Printed in China

9 8 7 6 5 4 3 2 1

CONTENTS

The grand, rose-red, rock-carved facade of The Treasury (Al-Khazneh), at Jordan's ancient archaeological site of Petra, a UNESCO World Heritage Site.

A Jordanian man in Amman wearing the *kaffiyeh*.

INTRODUCTION

FOR CENTURIES JORDAN WAS primarily a land of nomads. It was once located on the caravan route from the Arabian Peninsula to the Mediterranean Sea. It has no ancient metropolitan center, however, like those of its neighbors: Syria's Damascus, Saudi Arabia's Mecca and Medina, Iraq's Baghdad, Lebanon's Beirut, and Israel's Jerusalem. Historically, Jordan was part of Palestine and was never a "country" as one thinks of Syria and Egypt. The area west of the Jordan River has always been settled, while the harsh and largely uninhabited desert to the east has been used mostly for passage. The indigenous inhabitants traditionally considered themselves citizens of Greater Syria, Iraq, or the Hejaz (northwestern Saudi Arabia), while the Palestinians, for the most part 20th-century newcomers, dream of their own homeland. Of all the Arab countries, Jordan has had the closest relationship with Israel. It was the first—and remains the only—country among those in the Levant (the countries bordering the eastern Mediterranean Sea) and on the Arabian Peninsula to sign a peace treaty with Israel. It is also perhaps more religiously and culturally homogeneous than any of its neighbors except Saudi Arabia.

GEOGRAPHY

JORDAN BORDERS SAUDI ARABIA on the south and southeast, Israel and the territory of Palestine on the west, Syria on the north, and Iraq on the northeast. It also has a few miles of land near the Red Sea. It covers 35,000 square miles (90,650 square km), making it about the size of Kentucky in the United States.

GEOGRAPHICAL AREAS

Jordan can be divided into four geographical areas, each with its distinctive physical features.

THE JORDAN RIVER VALLEY This is the narrow, fertile valley of the Jordan River. It was here about 10,000 years ago that the earliest inhabitants abandoned their nomadic lifestyle and started to plant crops and build villages. Water-harnessing projects made agriculture possible, and by 3000 B.C. crops were being exported to neighboring regions. In the early 1970s new roads were built and irrigation projects such as the ambitious King Abdullah (formerly East Ghor) Canal were extended.

The area has hot, dry summers and short, mild winters—ideal conditions for cultivating certain crops. The average yearly rainfall is 12 inches (30 cm). The valley is situated along the country's western border with Israel and Palestine and is part of the Great Rift Valley, the largest fault system on earth, stretching 3,000 miles (4,830 km) from southwestern Syria to Mozambique in Africa. Unfortunately, the Jordan River Valley, which is considered to be the food bowl of Jordan, forms a meager 6 percent of the nation's land.

Above: **This lush spring is the largest of many found in the desertscape of the Wadi Rum.**

Opposite: **Cascading sand dunes on the stunning desert of the Wadi Rum National Reserve in Aqaba.**

7

THE DESERT The eastern and southern parts of Jordan receive less than 2 inches (5 cm) of annual rainfall. The desert makes up 80 percent of Jordan's land, which is mountainous and quite rugged in places (particularly in the south). The northern area of the desert consists of volcanic rock, while the southern part is wind-eroded granite and sandstone. A few oases—fertile areas where springs provide water and crops can be grown—are found scattered in the desert. The Jordanian desert is part of the Syrian Desert, the vast rocky badlands territory covering most of Syria, Jordan, Iraq, and part of northwestern Saudi Arabia.

WADI RUM Wadi Rum (WAH-dee ROOM) in southern Jordan is full of hilly rock formations. Wadi means "canyon" in Arabic, and the place is so named because the rugged hills make the flat land seem low, even though it is above sea level. Part of the 1962 movie *Lawrence of Arabia* was filmed there, and it was there, too, that Abdullah ibn Hussein, who later became king, organized the Bedouin troops that helped drive the Ottomans out of the country in 1918. Bedouins are nomadic Arabs living in the desert areas of several countries.

The canyon once provided fertile pastures for herds of grazing sheep. Today, only a handful of Bedouins live there in their goat-hair tents, depending mostly on tourists for their survival. Visitors come to enjoy the spectacular scenery and hiking or camping activities. The area is also the headquarters of the Desert Patrol Corps, or "camel" police. In an attempt to develop tourism, the government has, over the past several years, helped to sponsor an annual hot-air balloon event in Wadi Rum. The canyon was also declared a nature reserve in 1998. Since then, many steps have been taken in enhancing tourism while preserving the area's environment.

A wadi is a canyon in the desert where rain runs off the hills and soaks into the ground.
The surrounding area can be cultivated if farmers sink wells to reach the accumulated underground water.

HIGHLANDS The narrow land between the desert and the Jordan River Valley is a high plateau where the annual rainfall ranges from 13 inches (33 cm) in the north to 2 inches (5 cm) in the east and south. The climate in the highlands, like that in the Jordan River Valley, is Mediterranean, and many of the country's crops are grown there. Rainfall is unpredictable from year to year, and virtually all of it comes between November and May. Most years, before and after the rains, hot, dry winds blow in from the Arabian Peninsula, sometimes causing sandstorms.

MAJOR CITIES

Jordan's three largest cities—Amman, Zarqa, and Irbid—lie on the high plateau in the north. Ma'an lies farther south, and Aqaba is on the Gulf of Aqaba at the northeastern extremity off the Red Sea.

Since ancient times, the Bedouins have been able to use the poorest lands to their advantage. They camp for a few months at a time in one spot to graze their herds of goats, sheep, or camels. When the sparse fodder runs out, it is time to move on in search of more vegetation. When grazing their herds, the Bedouins do not always respect the limits set by national boundaries, and they sometimes get into trouble with governmental authorities for this practice.

The craggy and jagged hills of the Wadi Rum make it an impressive landmark in the vast Jordanian deserts.

At the beginning of the 20th century, Amman was little more than a village of a few hundred people. Its rapid growth began when it was declared capital of the newly independent nation of Transjordan in 1929.

AMMAN The capital city is also the country's largest city. It is the site of the ancient Ammonite capital of Rabbath Ammon. A millennium later it became the Greco-Roman city called Philadelphia. It had become a village of only a few hundred people in the 1800s when refugee Circassians "refounded" the city. The Circassians, who migrated from the Caucasus region of Russia, established businesses and introduced large-wheeled carts and a system of dirt roads. It was only when Abdullah, Jordan's first king, set up a government and built his first palace in Amman, however, that the city's importance was established.

The city's major growth began in 1948 with a flood of Palestinian refugees from the new state of Israel. Thousands more refugees arrived during the 1967 and 1973 Arab-Israeli wars and the Lebanese civil war. In 1991 there was an influx of Palestinians from the Gulf countries because they were expelled by the governments of those nations. Iraqis and Palestinians working in Kuwait and Iraq fled the Gulf War and found their way to Jordan. More recently, in 2003, a large number of Iraqis found refuge there after the new war in their homeland began.

According to 2006 estimates, Amman is home to more than 2.7 million people, or close to half of the country's estimated population of about 6 million, and functions as the nation's financial and cultural center. It is a bustling city spread over seven hills called *jabaal* (ja-BAL), most of which are connected by wide boulevards. Many international businesses are located in this city of beautiful Arab-Mediterranean architecture and modern high-rise buildings. Virtually all houses and other low structures are built from a light, honey-colored stone, most with carved embellishments and wrought iron or stone balustrades.

There are two major historical attractions in Amman. One, the ruins of a 6,000-seat Roman theater near the city center, is still used for various events. The other is the site of the Ammonite capital of Rabbath Ammon in biblical times. There are also numerous ethnic restaurants, art galleries, and museums such as the Folklore Museum, the Museum of Popular Traditions, and the Archaeological Museum.

The Roman theater was built in Amman in the second century A.D., when the city was called Philadelphia.

ZARQA Jordan's second-largest city, Zarqa has a population of more than 792,000, according to the 2000 census. It is a few miles northeast of Amman and has become a virtual suburb of the capital, forming its industrial zone. The city has an oil refinery and a tannery on its outskirts. Zarqa was established by the Circassians and Chechens.

IRBID Located only a few miles from the borders with Syria and Lebanon, Irbid is Jordan's third-largest city, with about 650,000 people. Artifacts and graves in the area show that it has been inhabited since the Bronze Age.

THE BLACK DESERT

One of the bleakest wastelands on earth exists in Jordan's northeastern desert. Consisting mostly of vast fields of sharp, rough, black lava rock, it is extraordinarily forbidding, unfit even for grazing sheep. This moonscape of volcanic mountains and smaller cinder cones extends into both Syria and Iraq and is the site of the ancient city of Jawa, the ruins of which can still be seen today. Bedouin superstition claims it is the land of the devil—*bilad ash shayton* (bi-LAUD ash SHY-ton)—and they call it "the stony land of walking men," in other words, fit only to pass through on the way to another place.

Sunbathing in Aqaba with rugged mountains as a backdrop. The city in the background is Elat in Israel.

Today it is the agricultural center of the country, located within a triangle formed by the Jordan, Zarqa, and Yarmuk rivers. Irbid is the site of Irbid-Yarmouk University.

MA'AN   One of Jordan's main cities, with fewer than 100,000 residents, Ma'an is located in the south near the end of the high plateau and the ruins of Petra. Ma'an is mainly a large sprawling town of settled and semisettled Bedouins. It is also the central Bedouin market for a very large area. It still plays as the gateway for Jordanians to pursue the hajj in neighboring Hejaz. The city is also a usual stopover for tourists venturing to the ancient city of Petra.

AQABA   The beauty of this place comes from its location at the head of the Gulf of Aqaba, which leads to the Red Sea, and being nestled in front of a semicircle of craggy desert mountains. It is a busy hub of economic activity, thanks to its large seaport, the only such port in Jordan. Fishing is carried out on a small scale. The area is modern and has facilities catering to the many tourists who arrive in summer, swelling its population to more than 70,000. The resorts along Aqaba's blue-water beaches are patronized by wealthy Arabs, as the site is only about 9 miles (15 km) from the Saudi Arabian border. Road and rail connections built in the late 1970s link it with Amman and boost its economy. Aqaba can also be reached by air on a daily basis using Royal Wings, a division of the Royal Jordanian Airlines.

THE GREAT RIFT VALLEY

This giant crack was formed during the Pleistocene epoch, 2.5 million years ago, when the African continental plate began to split. It is still expanding at the rate of about 0.04 inches (1 mm) a year, slowly pushing Africa away from the Arabian Peninsula. The Jordan River Valley, the Dead Sea, which is the lowest point on the earth's surface, the colorful cliffs of Petra, and the port of Aqaba are all found in the northern part of the Great Rift Valley. Near its southern end lies Lake Victoria, in east-central Africa, portrayed in the movie *The African Queen*.

CLIMATE

The dry season is between May and October, while most of the annual rains fall during winter, from November to April. The average temperature varies from summer highs of about 100°F (38°C) in the Dead Sea area to winter lows of below freezing in the north. Aqaba, the Red Sea port, experiences warm year-round temperatures ranging from 60°F to 90°F (16°C to 32°C). The high plateau is cooler in the north, with temperatures ranging from below freezing to about 86°F (30°C). The Jordan River Valley is moderate in winter and very hot in summer, reaching 100°F (38°C). On the other hand, the desert suffers extreme temperatures. In fact, regardless of the season, its climate is noteworthy for enormous variations between warm days and cold nights throughout the year, except for certain times when the nights are as hot as the day. The hottest temperature ever recorded in modern Jordan was in the Dead Sea region, reaching 124°F (51°C).

WATER BODIES

With growing populations in the region and with neighboring nations sharing common rivers, water is more important now than ever. Jordan has only three significant sources of freshwater: the Zarqa, Yarmuk, and Jordan rivers (it shares the latter two with its neighbors). Jordan borders the Red Sea through the Gulf of Aqaba. There is also the Dead Sea, the Azraq Oasis, and numerous small springs and seasonal oases. Agriculture consumes about 70 percent of all Jordan's water resources.

RIVERS The Jordan River rises from springs on the southwestern slopes of Mount Hermon (located on the boundaries between Lebanon, Israel, and Syria), 6,560 feet (2,000 m) above sea level. It has five separate tributaries along its course: the Dan, Hasbani, Banias, Zarqa, and Yarmuk rivers. The first three join the Jordan River in Israel near Lake Tiberias (the biblical Sea of Galilee).

The Yarmuk is the major tributary and forms the border between Jordan and Syria for 25 miles (40 km), and then the boundary of Israel and Jordan for a few miles before flowing into the Jordan River. Past this confluence, the Jordan River runs 68 miles (110 km), creating the border with Israel for 25 miles (40 km) before flowing entirely into Jordan, in a deep gorge called Ghor (part of the Great Rift Valley). It empties into the Dead Sea, but in recent years, due mostly to increasing use, water reaching the Dead Sea has dwindled to a mere trickle. The King Abdullah Canal, a man-made channel, delivers water from the Yarmuk River to Amman and its surroundings.

There are several small dams in this river system. A proposed dam on the Yarmuk was delayed for nearly a decade due to disputes among Syria, Jordan, and Israel over the distribution of water. Work finally began in 2004 to build the dam, which will provide electricity for Syria and a more dependable water source for Jordan. Jordan uses a substantial amount of water from both the Yarmuk and Zarqa rivers to irrigate its highland crops. Water shortages are common. In a land that is so arid, access to water is not a matter of politics alone, but also of life itself.

AZRAQ OASIS In eastern Jordan lies the extensive Azraq Oasis, the only permanent body of water in 46,000 square miles (119,000 square km) of desert. It provides refuge and water for thousands of animals.

THE DEAD SEA Imagine water so dense you cannot sink in it. That is the Dead Sea, a large inland sea with no outlet, so named by the Greeks, who noticed that its water was so salty that it could not support life. An annual evaporation rate of 80 inches (203 cm) keeps it highly saline, even though the Jordan River and small streams and springs feed it. The water is seven times saltier than ocean water. It contains a variety of salts: chlorine, bromide, sodium, sulfate, potassium, calcium, magnesium, carbonate, and silicate. These minerals form bizarre shapes that protrude from the water in some places. Numerous companies in Jordan and Israel (which also borders the sea) extract salt and other minerals from the sea for commercial purposes.

The Dead Sea is 46 miles (74 km) long and about 10 miles (16 km) wide. The surface of the water is 1,312 feet (400 m) below sea level, making it the lowest body of water on earth. Before 15,000 B.C. this sea was 200 miles (322 km) long. But around that time, the climate of the area became drier and hotter, and the sea began to evaporate and become saltier. In the mid-20th century, it shrank even more, its water level falling some 69 feet (21 m). The shrinking of the Dead Sea has reached crisis proportions. In May 2005 Israel, Palestine, and Jordan signed an agreement to pump water from the Red Sea into the Dead Sea via tunnels and canals in an attempt to restore it.

The biblical cities of Sodom and Gomorrah are thought to lie under the sea's southern waters, submerged by a catastrophic earthquake in the time of the Hebrew prophet Abraham. The Israelis call it the Salt Sea, while the Arabs call it the Sea of Lot—so named for

The lowest body of water in the world, the Dead Sea is one of Jordan's major waterways. It contains such a high concentration of salt that it crystallizes on its shores.

Purple irises bloom in the Jordan River Valley from February to May.

the biblical story of the destruction of Sodom and Gomorrah when Lot's wife turned to look longingly at the home she was fleeing and was transformed on the spot into a pillar of salt.

FLORA AND FAUNA

Despite its being mostly desert, Jordan supports a significant amount and variety of wildlife. There is also a growing amount of forested lands and plant life as a result of the government's forestation policy.

The Shaumari and Azraq wetlands are wildlife reserves watered by the Azraq Oasis. Animals found there include the Arabian oryx, gazelle, ostrich, hyena, mongoose, ibex (a wild goat), sand adder (a poisonous snake), and more than 300 bird species, including the white pelican, flamingo, crane, 15 species of duck, and seven species of egret. Other birds found in these reserves are the golden eagle, vulture, dove, and falcon. Many snakes, scorpions, and lizards also thrive in the desert.

The Red Sea divides into the shallow Gulf of Suez in the northwest and the mile-deep Gulf of Aqaba in the northeast. The Gulf of Aqaba has magnificent coral gardens inhabited by thousands of marine species, some of them unique to the area. Unfortunately, some of the coral and marine life has been dying in recent years due to pollution, overfishing, and heavy sea traffic to the Jordanian port of Aqaba and the nearby Israeli port of Elat. As a result, the Strategic Action Program for the Red Sea and Gulf of Aden has been developed by the countries around that area to help salvage and preserve marine life in the region.

Jordan has about 35,000 acres (14,000 ha) of forest, consisting largely of evergreen oak, pine, and olive trees. Many hardy olive trees grow wild, as they have for thousands of years. The government began a reforestation program in 1948, with only limited success. On Arbor Day in 2000, however, King Abdullah II planted a palm tree to kick off the first phase of a major Jordan River Valley forestation project, the planting of thousands of trees by hundreds of employees of the Ministry of Agriculture in an effort to "regreen" the valley. Some thorny plants as well as palm trees grow in the desert, particularly in wadis and oases. The most common flowers are poppies, roses, irises, and wild cyclamen.

A REAL UNICORN?

There is a belief that the mythical unicorn was modeled after the Arabian oryx, even though the latter has two straight, sharp horns instead of the single horn of the unicorn. The oryx, a type of antelope, has a striking appearance, and the Arabs cherish it for its beautiful dark eyes. Its Arabic name—*maha* (MAH-hah), a common name for women—means "crystal" and is inspired by the pure white fur of its body. Evolution has given the creature a characteristic that also belongs to camels—that of being able to live for extended periods in intense heat without food or water. This makes both animals ideally suited to life in the desert. Regrettably, as with many other creatures that have been able to adapt to harsh environments, the oryx has fallen prey to hunters. Most had been killed by the middle of the 20th century.

The Arabian Oryx World Herd Trustees was established in 1962 to restore the oryx to the wild, using zoo stock from around the world. Fourteen oryx were shipped from Oman, Germany, Switzerland, Saudi Arabia, and Qatar to three special zoos for breeding in the United States. When the Shaumari Reserve was completed in 1983, four male and four female oryx were shipped from the United States to Jordan. They have multiplied and are on their way to becoming a viable wild population again.

HISTORY

UNTIL THE EARLY 20TH CENTURY, Jordan was thought of as part of Greater Syria, an ancient land consisting of what is now Syria, Lebanon, Jordan, Israel, the territory of Palestine, and part of Turkey in the northwestern corner of the Arabian Peninsula. This region was part of an illustrious era reaching back 10,000 years. Greater Syria—or the Levant, as it is now called—is often referred to as "the cradle of Western civilization" and "the crossroads of civilizations."

ANCIENT HISTORY

Jordan is in the eastern part of what used to be Palestine. Its strategic site in the Middle East ensured that all the great early civilizations passed through the area, and its history was shaped by the Egyptians, Assyrians, Babylonians, Hittites, Greeks, and Romans. The land was fought over by these ancient peoples and contains some of the oldest known sites of civilization.

FIRST SETTLERS The first settlers were hunter-gatherers. Flints have been found in the Black Desert dating from the Stone Age, while prehistoric drawings of cows and bulls have been discovered in the desert and the Jordan River Valley. The valley is the location of crude settlements that originated around 8000 B.C., and there is evidence that the world's first wheat harvests were cultivated in this fertile area.

A city known to archaeologists as Jawa is the earliest known advanced settlement in Jordan, dating from the Middle Bronze Age (circa 4000 B.C.). This was a massive stone city built in the Black Desert by a people of

Above: **Ancient rock carvings found in the Wadi Rum indicate the presence of animals such as the horse and dog in prehistoric times.**

Opposite: **A local Bedouin guide stands in front of one of the ancient tombs of Petra.**

unknown origin who lived there for only about one generation. It is believed that they moved westward, because later settlements in the Jordan River Valley and throughout Palestine show the same water technology and building methods.

There are two main theories concerning the Jawaites and their origins. One is that they had moved from another urban culture in the east or north; the other is that they were local nomads who "invented" settled life. The first theory is considered the more likely. It is possible that they arrived in spring when runoff from the snow and rain in the nearby mountains looked promising, for there is usually no water there in summer.

SEMITIC PEOPLES AND THE PHILISTINES After the mysterious rise and fall of Jawa, many Semitic tribes occupied this region: Amorites, Canaanites, Hebrews, Ammonites, Moabites, Edomites, and Arameans. The Ammonites formed a capital city, called Rabbath Ammon, where Amman now stands. Around the 13th century B.C. an invasion of "peoples from

KITES IN THE SAND

Once prehistoric hunters and gatherers discovered ways to keep large numbers of animals at one site, permanent settlements could be built. Such was the case with what modern Bedouins call the "old men of Arabia."

In Jordan's eastern desert are the faintest remains—outlines, mostly—of kite-shaped corrals where wild (or semidomesticated) animals could be herded. The basic outlines are stone, but there is some evidence that posts and other materials may have been used to form the corrals and their long, funnel-shaped entrances. The exact age of the structures is not known, but some archaeologists think they were built by the Arab ancestors of present-day Bedouins.

JAWA—LOST CITY OF THE BLACK DESERT

Jawa must have been an imposing sight in the desolate landscape for anyone coming upon it. It covered about 30 acres (12 ha), most of it on a rise, in a wadi. A traveler approaching the city would have been impressed by its extensive planning. Outside the metropolis was a complex system of dams and canals, fed by winter runoff from the nearby mountains. The outer city walls were made of unworked stone set in rough courses with massive stone gates on stone hinges.

Inside the gates were flat-roofed huts with pounded mud floors, stone foundations, plastered walls, and wooden timbers supporting roofs of wooden slabs covered with mud-plastered reeds. The huts had stone benches along the interior walls, small pits in the floors, a hearth or two, and at least one round stone-lined storage bin—but no windows (with sweltering summers and freezing winters, and glass production still millennia away). Those who entered the massive, pentagon-shaped citadel then passed through another wall 20 feet (6 m) high and 13 to 16 feet (4 to 5 m) thick at the base. The houses here were larger than those outside, and each outbuilding of the citadel was divided into 24 cells with three traverse corridors. It could be concluded that the inner confines of the citadel were dwellings built for the elite.

One can only guess what other things visitors might have seen. Today, 6,000 years later, some sections of the inner wall still stand 20 feet (6 m) above the surrounding rock, and the cantilevered basalt slabs that held the roof of the corridors are still in place. This amazing architectural technology was contemporary with such feats as Stonehenge in England and the pyramids in Egypt. Today, Bedouins still use parts of the ancient water collection and storage system to water their camels and sheep.

the sea," believed to be the Philistines, took place. They settled on the coastal plain of what was then Canaan in an area that came to be known as the Plain of Philistia, from which the name Palestine is derived. By the late 11th century B.C., however, the Philistines found themselves threatened by the exodus of Israelites from Egypt, led by the prophet Moses.

Since then, the area's history has largely been that of invasion and conquest. Many of these settled groups were at constant war with one another over the use of water and the question of whose god was the "real" one. The warring peaked in the latter half of the second millennium B.C. when King David of the Hebrews attacked the Moabites and Edomites, slaying two-thirds of all Moabites and the entire male population of Edom. The northern part of the area was conquered by outsiders: the Assyrians around 900 B.C., the Babylonians under King Nebuchadnezzar, and then the Persians. The Egyptians, too, controlled the area for a time.

A Roman triumphal arch built in Jerash in A.D. 129.

NABATEANS   Even when the Assyrians and other conquerors came, they only controlled the northern part of the land that is now Jordan. The Nabateans ruled southern Jordan, part of the northwestern Arabian Peninsula, Palestine, and present-day Syria for about 1,000 years, until they were defeated by the Roman general Trajan in A.D. 106. The Nabateans are often described as a people of Arab origin. They were primarily spice merchants who plied their trade along the "spice trail" from the Far East, dealing with Persians, Hebrews, Ptolemeans, and Seleucideans (the latter two were early Greeks).

Their successes can be attributed, as with the Jawaites, to their water technology in an arid climate. They developed an extensive system of large cisterns built to collect rainwater and to melt snow, making the desert habitable. These cisterns still exist today in the form of huge square caves measuring more than 100 feet (30 m) on each side. The openings were small and covered, marked with signs known only to the Nabateans.

THE ROMANS   The Romans made this region part of their empire for several hundred years before and after the beginning of the current era, and left behind numerous ruins. Jerash (north of Amman), for example, is sometimes called the Pompeii of the East, and while it is one of the best-preserved Roman sites in Asia, it was also influenced by the Greeks. The Romans brought commercial success and innovation to the area, but as their rule began to disintegrate, the chaos of tribal warfare once more took hold. It was during this chaos that the most powerful force in the history of the Middle East swept in—Islam.

PETRA, THE ROSE-COLORED CITY

The pinnacle of Nabatean civilization, from about the fourth century B.C. to the second century A.D., is still visible today in the ancient city of Petra. With an ample supply of fresh spring water, the city became a major stopping point on the caravan route from Arabia to the Mediterranean.

Petra is a city of elaborate facades in a combination of unique Nabatean and Greco-Roman architectural styles. They were carved into reddish-purple sandstone cliffs (leading to the name "rose-colored city") hundreds of feet high in a network of canyons that are part of the Great Rift Valley. Behind the often enormous front faces of the cliffs are relatively small, square rooms. The city was ideal for protection from enemies, since the main entrance was through the *siq* (SEEK), a narrow, winding cleft in the sandstone. Its high elevation of 2,700 feet (820 m) above sea level and its location at the bottom of the gorges made it a cool place to live in summer. In winter, it sometimes snows on the heights, while there is no snow at the bottom of the canyons.

During the Arab uprising against the Ottoman Turks in World War I (WWI), Petra was the site of a famous battle in which Lawrence of Arabia fought. Today, some Bedouins who service tourists live in the caves.

MIDDLE HISTORY

The soul of modern Jordan was formed during the centuries of Arab rule when Arabic became the common language and Islam the dominant religion. However, many Christians and Jews remained in the area throughout the emergence of Jordan.

OMAYYADS After the death of the Prophet Muhammad in A.D. 632, his followers continued to spread his teachings. In the middle of the eighth century, the Omayyads, the strongest of the clans from the Hejaz, overran Greater Syria and established their headquarters in Busra, just north of what is now the Jordanian-Syrian border. From there they conquered and ruled the entire Arabian Peninsula, northern Africa, and parts of southern Europe—an area about the size of the former Roman Empire.

Although the area that is now Jordan was not of great importance in the Arabian empire, the Arab rulers built magnificent palaces and hunting lodges there, and the ruins of them still remain. The Arabian empire lasted for several hundred years, and its linguistic, cultural, and religious legacy lives on today, nearly 1,000 years later. As Arab dominance declined, tribes and clans once again ruled their own small pieces of land in what is now Jordan. Unlike the territory that is now Syria, where the Omayyads established a continuing tradition of urban life, the area of Jordan remained rural and nomadic.

OTTOMANS In the mid-16th century, the Ottoman Turks took over the Levant and the Arabian Peninsula. As with the previous empire, Jordanian land was not very important to the Ottomans except as a passage from the north to the holy cities of Islam—Mecca and Medina. The Ottomans named the land Transjordan, indicating its primary use as a land corridor. (The British, the last outsiders to dominate the country, also used the Ottoman name.)

The Ottomans were strict overlords who imposed taxes and adopted a military style of governance. They allowed local administration of the territory by Arabs loyal to them, but there was a lack of social and economic development. Although there was order in the cities, the outlying areas were plagued by lawlessness. The Ottomans ruled for about 400 years, until the end of WWI, when they were driven out of Arab lands in large part by Bedouins living in Jordan and the Hejaz, backed by the British. Abdullah ibn Hussein I, the man who later was to become king of Jordan and great-grandfather of today's King Abdullah II, led the troops who were responsible for the first major Arab victory over the Ottomans.

THE 20TH CENTURY

In order to understand the conflicts in this region, it is important to understand their causes. After the Turks were driven out, France and Britain—the winning European powers of WWI—bargained with each other to take over the land of the Levant for political, religious, and economic reasons. This self-interest, combined with ignorance of the cultures involved, led to the parceling out of Greater Syria into what would become the countries of Syria, Lebanon, Jordan, Israel, and the territory of Palestine today.

IN LIMBO The new League of Nations approved the partitioning of Greater Syria in 1923. Long before that, however, France had taken over what is now Syria and Lebanon, while Britain had taken over Palestine and Transjordan (present-day Israel, the territory of Palestine, and Jordan).

The principle of the League of Nations's mandate was that Britain would help develop the area commercially and politically. Britain had various interests in the area. These were to safeguard its route to India via the Suez Canal, maintain access to a cheap source of oil from what is now Iraq, uphold its power in the Mediterranean, expand its commercial and financial interests, and create a homeland for European Jews in Palestine.

The British sent political officers to three Jordanian communities to deliver several assurances. One was that the Jordanians would receive assistance in organizing local government; another was that Transjordan would not be annexed to Palestine; and the third was that Britain would not conscript residents for military service nor disarm them. Because of these assurances, Arab nationalists were at first in favor of the British presence and regarded it as protection from the French military forces in the north.

THE FIRST LEADER Abdullah ibn Hussein I was born in Mecca in 1882 to a *sharif* (SHAH-rif), an Arab noble descended from the Prophet Muhammad. He spent part of his childhood and early adult years in Istanbul, where his father was a ranking Arab in the Ottoman administration.

Abdullah and his brother Faisal had great dreams, but Abdullah's were perhaps the more grandiose: he wished to rule all the land that is now Syria, Jordan, Iraq, and northwestern Saudi Arabia (the Hejaz). The British actually recognized him as the king of Iraq for a short time to protect their commercial interests there. However, when the French drove Faisal, who had been crowned king of Syria, out of Damascus, the British "gave" Faisal the throne in Iraq, thus firming up their interests in the region with

two apparently loyal leaders. The two brothers, meanwhile, had used the British against the Ottomans and later maintained the alliance for their own protection as well as for financial and other support.

Winston Churchill, Britain's foreign minister at the time, liked Abdullah from the beginning and convinced him to move to Amman from Ma'an in southern Jordan, where the future king had based himself while hoping to take over the Hejaz. Abdullah agreed to Churchill's request and set up his first headquarters in the home of a prominent Circassian.

THE BEGINNINGS OF MODERN JORDAN Under British control, Transjordan became a state in April 1921. In October 1922, Abdullah went to London, where he and British officials established the borders of the new nation, and he was officially made emir, or ruler, in late 1923. Britain pushed for a constitutional monarchy with an elected legislature, but Abdullah balked for the time being.

Abdullah ibn Hussein I meets British Foreign Minister Ernest Bevin. Abdullah had the support of the British from the time he sought to drive out the Ottoman rulers to the time that Transjordan was established and when Jordan gained its independence. His reliance on Britain often placed him at odds with other Arab rulers.

Abdullah was a nomad at heart, and despite the construction of his first palace in the mid-1920s, he still camped in his goat-hair tent for weeks at a time, moving throughout the country to build rapport with the Bedouins and win their loyalty. This started a tradition that continues to this day and has tied Bedouin loyalty to the crown. The country's first army consisted almost completely of Bedouins, and even today they form the majority of those serving in the army.

ZIONISTS, REFUGEES, AND TURMOIL Britain's Balfour Declaration of 1917 (which became part of the League of Nations's mandate) guaranteed the Jews a homeland within Palestine if they wished to move there. This caused immense turmoil there and in surrounding areas as militant Zionists began arriving. Their stated goal was to take over all the land they considered holy to Judaism. The Palestinian people, who had lived there for more than 1,000 years, rebelled against the unwelcome settlers, and violence soon escalated on both sides. The ensuing conflicts pushed some Palestinians into Transjordan, but the worst was yet to come. The first serious rebellion against the League's mandates occurred in the mid-1920s in Syria with the brutal French reaction that drove many Arab nationalists into Transjordan, as did the Hejazi civil war, which was then raging in northwestern Arabia. Then, after a devastating earthquake hit Amman in 1927, the Jews in Palestine helped to rebuild the city.

Abdullah saw an opportunity for himself in this Jewish involvement and offered to support the development of a Jewish homeland if the World Zionist Organization would use its influence to help him become king of a combined Transjordan-Palestine. This resulted in Jews actually buying land from Transjordan landowners and becoming settlers in the country.

With this historical backdrop, a formal Transjordan-Anglo agreement in 1928 resulted in a constitution that was unsatisfactory to most local residents, igniting various demonstrations. Once calm had returned, it was not long until another major upheaval began.

In 1936 Palestinian peasants held a six-month general strike that included an armed uprising against the immigration of Zionist settlers to their homeland. The settlers were supported by the British mandate. The revolt that ensued was defeated by a union of the British army and Zionist militias. As a result of this revolt, which lasted until 1939, the Palestinians did not put up much resistance when they were finally evicted from their homeland between 1947 and 1948. Thereafter, a great number of such evicted Palestinians settled in the Transjordan, thus further increasing the Arab refugee population of the land.

WAR AND INCREASED INDEPENDENCE In February 1946 Abdullah went to London to negotiate independence. Within a month a treaty was signed, but the weak new country was still heavily dependent on British military and financial support. In March 1946 a constitution giving almost complete power to Abdullah was adopted, and on May 25 his lifelong dream was realized when he crowned himself king—Abdullah ibn Hussein I. The revised constitution also gave the country its modern name—Jordan.

The formation of Israel was the bedrock of all the troubles to follow, for at the last moment of resistance against being evicted from their homeland, the Arabs of Palestine (Palestinians) were attacked severely by Zionist militias. This was the end of a process that took half a century— the Palestinian displacement from the region. By the time the British withdrew from Palestine, Israel as a nation was declared and soon after was confronted by the Arab League, in which Jordan was a member. The League confronted the newly established state because it wanted to salvage parts of this region (Palestine), which had been annexed by

ZIONISM

In 1878 Jews bought farmland in what was then Palestine. Their aim was to set up a community. At that time, there was much persecution of the Jews in eastern Europe. In 1897 Theodor Herzl created the World Zionist Organization. Waves of immigrants entered Palestine and set up agricultural settlements throughout the country. During WWI, the British foreign secretary, Arthur James Balfour, declared that his government favored "the establishment in Palestine of a national home for the Jewish people." This led to the promise of British assistance embodied in the Balfour Declaration. The problem in Palestine today stems from the fact that this decision displaced millions of native Arabs who had made

this land their home for the past thousand years. Thus, while Zionism ensured a home for the landless nation (global Jewry), it overlooked the impact that such moves would make on the native populace.

the Israeli army, for their displaced Palestinian brethren. This year also furthered the cause for Jordanian independence through a revision of the Transjordan-Anglo treaty. As a result of these two events, hundreds of Palestinian villagers were killed and many others expelled. The exodus flooded Jordan with homeless Palestinians. (About 3 million Palestinians are today registered as refugees or displaced persons in Jordan.) The armistice at the end of the 1948 war left the West Bank (the land west of the Jordan River) unclaimed by Israel. This land between Israel and Jordan came under Jordanian jurisdiction until a solution for it could be made. Hence, Jordan had the job of policing the border between the West Bank and Israel.

In December 1949 Abdullah effectively annexed the West Bank, setting up parliamentary elections—the first in the new country—to give credibility to his annexation. The new parliament approved the land grab, but that was its only action, as Abdullah dissolved the body soon after. The Palestinians of the West Bank acquiesced for lack of a better alternative.

The king was assassinated in Jerusalem in July 1951. His grandson Hussein, who became the third king of Jordan, was with him at the time and was hit by a bullet. A chest medal he was wearing caught the bullet and saved his life.

In 1950 the population of Jordan's East Bank was only 476,000, while there were nearly a million Palestinians in the West Bank, which had just become part of Jordan. After Abdullah's death, with no appointed or apparent successor, Jordan's political leaders were paralyzed. Some wanted to form a union with Iraq, a few wanted Abdullah's son Talal to be crowned, while many others wanted Talal (who had both mental and physical disabilities) to step aside and allow his underage son, Hussein, to be crowned.

A SHORT-TERM KING While the political battles raged, Talal was incommunicado in a Swiss sanitarium. When his doctors declared him healthy in August 1951, he returned to Amman, where his half brother Nayif was planning a coup. Knowledge of the coup reached the government, security was tightened, and the coup failed. Talal refused to step aside and allow his son to be crowned, so his coronation took place on September 6, 1951.

Talal soon became increasingly violent toward his wife and children. Before long the deterioration in his health became so obvious that the country's cabinet decided to seek his hospitalization. Around this time the king made a trip to the United States, and a "throne council" was formed in Amman. Jordan's prime minister then was a strong leader who convinced Talal to return to Jordan for hospitalization, leaving the throne council in charge until Hussein came of age. Then, in August 1952, the parliament voted to depose the sick king and crown the young Hussein. In September, Talal went to Egypt for treatment before moving to Istanbul, where he spent the rest of his life. He died in 1972.

A THIRD KING In December 1952 a new, more democratic constitution was adopted, and in May 1953 Hussein was crowned. The young King Abdullah II, who had been educated at Harrow in Britain, was only 16 years old. The new king's mother, Zayn, was a strong woman, powerful behind the scenes, and had helped oust her incapacitated husband and get her son crowned. She continued to exercise much influence in Jordanian affairs.

The first few years of King Hussein's rule were rocky. There were constant low-level border skirmishes between Jordan and Israel, and he had problems with power-hungry prime ministers. Also, he was vehemently anticommunist and wanted to join the Baghdad pact along with Turkey and Iraq, but the populace wanted a socialist government, such as Egypt's or Syria's, and was violently opposed to the pact. The king gave in to the opposition but then dissolved parliament, hoping to set up a more compliant one. Riots, strikes, and overwhelming opposition to the parliamentary dissolution caused the king to reverse his decision. These things brought the country close to collapse, for as the Saudi troops amassed near the southern border, curfews and martial law were imposed, and Britain was prepared to send in paratroopers to support the Jordanian government. Britain's aid to Jordan lasted until the Egyptian takeover of the Suez Canal in 1956, after which King Hussein appealed for and won support from the United States. Thereafter, his leadership position was consolidated, although far from trouble free.

STRIVING FOR IDENTITY In early 1958, Syria and Egypt united to form the United Arab Republic. They were socialist countries friendly toward the Soviet Union and its allies. Because of King Hussein's strong anticommunist disposition, he was considered an enemy of both countries, and Syria closed its border with Jordan. At the same time, Iraq and Jordan

united to form the Arab Federation, but this did not last because a socialist revolution in Iraq in July of the same year quickly ended the union.

At the time of the Iraqi revolution, and again two years later, assassination plots were uncovered against King Hussein. From 1959 to 1961 there were several more attempts on his life. Thereafter, things appeared to settle down for a while, with peace being made with Egypt in 1961. This was followed by an increase in national prosperity.

In 1957, however, the government, under Prime Minister Sulayman Nabulsi, posed a challenge for the monarchy when it was suspected to have maneuvered around the monarchy on certain political agendas such as obtaining aid from the Soviet Union. This made King Hussein uneasy, and as political tensions increased, he demanded the resignation of this government. This started the ball of turmoil to begin its roll downhill to chaos. In 1963 Syria, Iraq, and Egypt signed an agreement for the formation of a loose union, which unleashed massive demonstrations in Jordan both for and against the union. The turmoil became so great that King Hussein dissolved parliament and declared martial law. These royal crackdowns, however, did not bring peace to the country.

JORDANIAN HISTORY UNTIL GULF WAR OF 1991

1200 B.C.	Ammonites form capital city of kingdom—Rabbath Ammon—where Jordan's capital Amman now stands.
800 B.C.	Arab Nabeteans move into what is now southern Jordan and build Petra.
200 B.C.	Greeks occupy area and build city of Philadelphia in region that is now Amman.
A.D. 106	Romans defeat Nabateans and add their own buildings and infrastructure at Petra; they also build the city of Jerash in what is now northern Jordan.
Mid-1500s	Ottoman Turks take over the Levant and the Arabian Peninsula.
1800s	Circassian refugees from Russia settle in Amman, establish businesses, and introduce large-wheeled carts and system of dirt roads.
1917	Great Britain's Balfour Declaration guarantees Jews a homeland in Palestine (west of the Jordan River); militant Zionists begin to arrive, causing turmoil and pushing first Palestinian refugees into Transjordan; Ottomans driven from the Levant and the Arabian Peninsula by allies and Bedouin armies; Great Britain takes over land that is now Palestine, Israel, Jordan, and Iraq.
1921	Transjordan officially becomes semi-independent.
1922	Abdullah and British officials create borders of new nation.
1923	Newly formed League of Nations approves Great Britain's trusteeship with mandate that it would help develop area politically and economically; Abdullah is made emir (ruler).
1946	Independence gained from Great Britain; new constitution gives Abdullah nearly total control of country; Abdullah crowns himself king.
1948	Nation of Israel established; surrounding Arab countries immediately attack it; large numbers of Palestinians are killed and expelled, flooding Jordan with refugees.
1949	Abdullah annexes Palestinian part of West Bank.
1951	Abdullah is assassinated in Jerusalem; Abdullah's mentally troubled son Talal is crowned.
1952	In August, Jordan's parliament votes to depose the infirm Talal and crown his son Hussein; a more democratic constitution adopted.
1953	Hussein, only 16 years old, is crowned king.
1958	Jordan and Iraq join to form the Arab Federation, but revolution in Iraq ends union later in year.
1963	Syria, Iraq, and Egypt sign an agreement for a loose union. There are demonstrations in Jordan for and against the move, and King Hussein dissolves parliament.
1964	Palestinian Liberation Organization (PLO) establishes the Palestinian National Charter in Jerusalem, sets up its headquarters in Amman.

JORDANIAN HISTORY UNTIL GULF WAR OF 1991 (*continued from previous page.*)

1965	Tensions rise between King Hussein and PLO over latter's use of Jordan as an attack base against Israel. Jordanian army kills a PLO commando after PLO raid on Israel.
1966	Hussein closes PLO offices in Amman.
1967	Israeli attack on Jordanian village (reprisal for PLO attack from Jordan) destroys village and kills or injures 60 Jordanians, setting off 1967 Arab-Israeli war. Israel takes West Bank from Jordan, and Arab world mourns loss of Jerusalem, Islam's second most holy city, to Israel.
1967–68	Jordanian-based PLO action against Israel results in Israeli reprisals against Jordanian villages and creates internal pressure to control PLO. Jordanian army kills 28 PLO commandos.
1970	"Black September." Civil war breaks out—including battles with Syria, which supports PLO—and all commandos are killed, arrested, or driven out of the country.
1973	Another Arab-Israeli war starts. Jordan does not fight but sends troops and equipment to help Syria. More Palestinian refugees flood into Jordan.
1980–83	War with Syria narrowly averted. Cause of trouble is King Hussein's support of Islamic militants trying to overthrow Syrian government. Arab League intervenes. Hussein meets Syrian president and promises to stop his country's support for insurgents.
1984	Hussein recalls parliament. Parliament convenes for first time in 21 years.
1986	New electoral law is passed, creating small constituencies—Christians, Palestinians, and Circassians/Chechens. Palestinians in refugee camps also given representation.
1988	Hussein formally cedes Jordan's claim on West Bank to Palestinians.
1989	First parliamentary election is held in 22 years (since 1967).
1991	Gulf War breaks out. Jordan remains neutral and is flooded with refugees from Iraq and Palestinians from Kuwait.

TOWARD MODERN TIMES

In 1973 another Arab-Israeli war broke out and more Palestinian refugees flooded into Jordan. From 1980 to 1983 war with Syria was narrowly averted over King Hussein's support of Islamic militants' trying to overthrow the Syrian government. The Arab League (a council of the leaders of the Arab nations) intervened. The king met the Syrian president and pledged to stop his country's support of the Syrian insurgents.

In 1989, with relative peace and the severing of the West Bank from Jordan the year before, the country held its parliamentary election for the

King Hussein is the Father of Modern Jordan. The country was a backwater of the Arab world when he came to power, but by the time of his death in 1999, Jordan had risen through tough times and is now one of the most modern nations in the region.

first time since 1967, paving the way for the Palestinians to stake their claim on the disputed area. For a time, Jordan prospered, but the Gulf War broke out in 1991. Jordan remained neutral but lost its aid from both Western countries and the rich Arab Gulf states.

In 1994, after several years of secret negotiations supported by the governments and diplomats of several Western countries, Jordan and Israel declared that they could coexist peacefully.

CHANGE OF MONARCHS

In 1999, after several years of illness, King Hussein died. Only a few days later, his eldest son, Abdullah II (whose mother is British), ascended the throne. The nation mourned greatly for King Hussein, as he was not only the longest-running ruler of Jordan but was also responsible for bringing the country into the modern era and keeping some semblance of balance and harmony among his people.

NEW ELECTORAL LAWS

Jordan's attempts at a more democratic society have waxed and waned, mostly due to the justifiable fears of antigovernment violence. For example, in 1989 the first parliamentary elections in 22 years were held, and then, a new elections law that granted multiparty democracy for the first time in 37 years was passed in 1993. Only four years later, however, laws that restricted freedom of the press were passed, and Islamist political parties boycotted legislative elections on the ground that they were unfair to Islamists. Then in 2001 the parliament's term expired without

THE PALESTINIAN LIBERATION ORGANIZATION

In 1964 the Palestinian Liberation Organization (PLO) was formed officially in Jerusalem, half of which at that time was part of Jordan. Shortly after establishing its headquarters in Amman, the PLO faced a rocky relationship with Jordan's government. By 1965 tension was rising between King Hussein and the PLO over the latter's use of Jordan as a base to attack Israel. Israel wanted to control the West Bank and to halt a combined Egyptian-Syrian nationalist influence in the region. So the Israelis attacked a number of Jordanian villages that housed PLO's main command posts. As a result, King Hussein closed the PLO office in Amman for fear that the organization was making Jordan a target for Israel. The PLO attacks initialed the start of the Arab-Israeli war of 1967, which lasted for six days. The final victor was Israel. As a result of the victory over the Arab world, Israel took the West Bank from Jordan. The aftermath resulted in another mass movement of Palestinian refugees into Jordan, creating internal pressure on the government to control the PLO. All this time, the organization's support base was growing by leaps and bounds. It attracted many Arabs from neighboring Arab countries to fight for its cause, replacing the role of several Arab governments.

A Jordanian-based PLO action against Israel in 1968 caused Israeli reprisals against Jordanian villages in what would be remembered by both Jordanians and Palestinians as the Battle of Karameh. The PLO realized that it could not depend on aid from Arab countries as it set out to fight its battles in guerrilla warfare. These included surprise raids on Israeli settlements and terrorist acts against government installations and citizens of Western countries that heavily supported Israel at the expense of the Palestinian people.

This created a formidable challenge for the Jordanian government, as local support was polarized between PLO and Jordan's government, further challenging the government's legitimacy. Since the Israeli counterattacks were centered on Jordan, the PLO's political homeland, the government saw the strained international relations as being intolerable. This tension mounted to a civil war, which broke out between the PLO and the Jordanian army. As a result, in September 1970, King Hussein expelled the PLO from his country in a period that is known to Palestinians as Black September.

new elections because the government feared that sympathy for the Palestinian's new conflict with Israel would give Islamist parties a victory. In the next parliamentary elections (2003), the new king's supporters won a majority of the seats, while the Islamist parties got only 18 seats.

GOVERNMENT

JORDAN'S OFFICIAL NAME is the Hashemite Kingdom of Jordan. Despite its past turmoil and long-term suspension of parliament and civil liberties, it is generally considered to have the most democratic government in the Arab world today. Its bureaucracy, though huge (nearly half of all employed citizens work for the government), is one of the most efficient and least corrupt in the Arab world.

GOVERNMENT STRUCTURE

The monarch is the head of state, while a prime minister appointed by the king heads

the day-to-day affairs of government. The prime minister appoints a cabinet. The prime minister and members of the cabinet are subject to parliamentary approval.

The legislative assembly, or parliament, has 142 members and is divided into two houses: the Senate, whose members are appointed by the king, and a house of representatives, the House of Deputies, whose members are elected by popular vote. A term of office is four years. All citizens over 18 (except members of the royal family) can vote, including Palestinians in refugee camps, as they are granted citizenship. The monarch signs and executes or vetoes all laws passed by the parliament, as well as any constitutional amendments.

Under the central government are five territorial districts called *muhafaza* (mu-HAH-fah-zah), each headed by a governor appointed by the minister of the interior. Under the district governments are cities and towns, each with an elected mayor and council responsible for local affairs.

Above: **In Jordan, women participate actively in politics, as seen in this parliamentary elections campaign.**

Opposite: **The fourth king of Jordan, King Abdullah II, at a formal state event.**

When the late King Hussein assumed the throne in 1953, he inherited a poor and divided country. Years later, however, he had succeeded in building an independent nation with its own identity.

THE MONARCH

Unlike most countries with royal leaders who inherit centuries or millennia of family rule, Jordan's royalty is a creation of 20th-century forces, specifically British will and the overpowering personal desire of Abdullah ibn Hussein to be king. This situation is unique to the Muslim world, where being descended from the Prophet Muhammad is all that it takes to qualify as a supreme ruler. Abdullah's father (the great-great grandfather of today's King Abdullah II) was such a leader—but not in the territory that is now Jordan.

Jordan's kings have claimed (and most Arabs accept) that they are descendants of the Prophet Muhammad via the house of Hashem from the tribe of Quraish (ku-RAYSH)—hence, the country's official name, the Hashemite Kingdom of Jordan. Their ancestry is one of the reasons that they have remained in power in a land that, a mere three generations earlier, their family was not part of.

KINGS, CITIZENS, AND DEBTS

King Hussein was known for his largesse, accepting citizens' personal requests at his palaces. Such requests were most often from the poorest, least important citizens. Appeals too onerous were dismissed, but most were granted. This made the recipients and their families indebted to and supportive of the king. Likewise, King Hussein considered himself in debt to anyone harmed by a member of the royal family and invited them to make a request for recompense (compensation for personal injury is a common characteristic of Arab culture). Most people ask only for something simple, such as a photograph of themselves with the king.

It appears that King Abdullah II is continuing these traditions, endearing himself to the public in the process.

The scholar Linda Layne's description of the concept of nation is a very appropriate statement for Jordan's situation: "Because spaces, whether domestic or national, are defined by people and not by places, they are not permanent or fixed. It is the social action of individuals that makes both house and homeland." Only a few decades ago, Jordan was little more than a barren wasteland with a few Bedouin tribes grazing their sheep. So, to a large extent, it is through the social actions of the previous monarch that it has become a genuine nation. King Hussein was a man with modern ideas who believed in diplomacy instead of military action. Although his government was repressive at times, he felt that such action was necessary to stave off anarchy in his nation.

Although the first-born son of a king or queen traditionally accedes to the throne, King Hussein originally selected his younger brother Hassan as crown prince. There can only be speculation as to why he did this, but one possibility is that, due to several attempts that had been made on his life, the king did not want to risk leaving the country in the hands of an infant. Nevertheless, on January 25, 1999, just before his death, King Hussein decreed his eldest son, Abdullah II, as the new crown prince. Less than two weeks later, only hours after the death of Hussein, Abdullah was crowned king.

WESTERN QUEENS IN THE DESERT

Muslim men, by law and custom, are allowed to have up to four wives. King Hussein married four women, but only one at a time. It is believed that he divorced his first wife, Dina Abdul Hamed (an Arab), because she tried to become politically powerful at his expense. After the divorce, the king traveled a great deal in Europe, where he met and eventually married a British woman, Toni Gardner. She converted to the Islamic faith, took the name Muna, and bore the king four children.

In 1973 King Hussein divorced Muna and almost immediately announced his engagement to a beautiful young Jordanian Palestinian, Alia Toukan, who worked for Royal Jordanian Airlines. Jordanians were extremely upset, as Queen Muna had been popular with most of them, and the king was criticized harshly in the press—not for marrying the younger woman, but for divorcing the older one.

In the winter of 1977, Queen Alia was killed in a helicopter crash in the hills of the Jordan River Valley. The king mourned her loss, but just a year later, he met a Princeton-educated American named Lisa Halaby, who had ancestors from Allepo in Syria. They were married a few months

The late King Hussein with his American wife, Queen Noor al-Hussein, married in 1978. The queen undertook many social improvements.

later, after she had converted to Islam and was renamed Noor al-Hussein, or Light of Hussein. For the second time, an Arab country had a queen from the West, and both queens endeared themselves to the citizens.

MINORITY GROUP REPRESENTATION

Jordan's electoral laws guarantee that minority groups are represented in the government. First, the constitution outlaws any discrimination based on race, language, or religion. Heads of state and prime ministers, however, must be Muslim. This is not unreasonable, considering that as much as 95 percent of the populace is Muslim. Christians, who make up only 3 to 4 percent of Jordan's population, are accorded nine legislative members. The country's Circassians and Chechens are granted one legislative seat for every 5,000 citizens (making a total of three seats). Six legislative seats are also reserved for women. Bedouins, who mostly still live a traditional nomadic lifestyle, account for only 1 percent of the population but are also guaranteed legislative representation. Even Palestinians in refugee camps are granted representation in parliament.

A Jordanian Muslim woman casts her vote in the country's first parliamentary elections since King Abdullah's ascension to the throne in 1999.

Although such representation might seem unfair to the majority, it is the king's and the government's way of protecting the rights and interests of small groups against an often volatile majority.

Jordanian military and police officers marching in a graduation ceremony of the 19th Military and Police Sciences Classes of Mu'ta University in the city of Karak in 2006.

LAW, ORDER, AND PROTECTION

Jordan's military, police, and legal systems are based on modern British models.

MILITARY The Jordanian army has about 75,000 members, divided among the air force, the naval coast guard, and the "people's militia," in which women can serve. This is one of the smallest militaries in the Middle East and is only a fraction of the size of Syria's military organizations, which have more than a million members. Despite its small size, Jordan's military absorbs one-quarter of the national budget. It is well trained and dedicated to the government. The king is the commander in chief. In 1999 the conscription of men 18 years or older was abolished, so now the military consists only of volunteers. Women may also volunteer for noncombat positions.

SECURITY FORCES The regular police force is modern and limited in authority by the constitution, but Jordan, like some Arab countries, also has a "secret" police that can infiltrate and control groups the government feels are a threat to its survival. In the past, this force was brutally repressive, engaging in torture, midnight arrests, and even murder. The three agents of national security are the military, the Public Security Directorate (PSD), and the General Intelligence Directorate (GID), all of which have been responsible for such abuses to some degree. The GID, formed since 1964, serves a function somewhat similar to the U.S. FBI. Since the early

1990s, these organizations have been reined in substantially; however, old habits die hard, and abuses still exist.

"CAMEL" POLICE Jordan has a special police branch called the Desert Patrol, or Camel Corps, whose function is to patrol the desert, giving assistance to its nomadic dwellers. It was established in 1931 to help keep peace among warring tribes, but today, with a decline in the traditional Bedouin lifestyle, it exists more out of tradition than from real need. They still lead special parades wearing attractive uniforms, but normally these police wear khaki uniforms and traditional Arab red-and-white headdresses called *kaffiyeh* (kah-FEE-yay), and carry handcrafted silver daggers in silver scabbards. Today, the Camel Corps has about 1,000 members.

THE LEGAL SYSTEM The king appoints judges, and there are three categories of courts: civil, religious, and special. These include the Supreme Court, Muslim and Christian courts to address personal matters such as inheritance and marriage, and special courts to resolve land, municipal, tax, and customs issues.

A member of the Bedouin Desert Police in Petra.

The legal system protects the interests of Jordan's minority citizens. Christians have their own courts for personal and civic matters, and the ancient tribal laws of the Bedouins take precedence over the national legal system in their own affairs. The Circassians and Chechens use the Muslim courts. Jordan's laws are based in part on Islamic precepts (particularly in courts for Muslims), but Jordan does not follow Shari'a law, the legal system based on Islamic law, as do Saudi Arabia and a few other predominantly Muslim countries.

45

ECONOMY

JORDAN HAS FEW NATURAL RESOURCES, land that is largely too dry for raising crops, and industries that are mostly newly developed, yet it has achieved a moderately strong, modern economy and is beginning to support itself financially. It also receives extensive financial aid from Great Britain and the United States. Since he was enthroned in 1999, King Abdullah II has instituted numerous economic reforms.

After Jordan's loss of the West Bank to Israel during the 1967 Arab-Israeli war, there were fears that its economic development would be impeded. It has overcome the setback, however, and the country's economy continues to expand. In 1990 Jordan's per capita gross domestic product (GDP) was $1,340; it fell to $968 following the Gulf War in 1991 but grew to about $1,817 in 2003, and in 2005 was estimated at about $4,200. This does not compare with neighboring Israel's estimated per capita GDP of $24,600 in the same year, but Jordanians still enjoy a fairly high standard of living. The country has the third-largest stock market in the Arab world, after Kuwait.

Although oil is yet to be found in significant amounts (it supports less than 1 percent of Jordan's own oil consumption), natural gas reserves found in 1987 in northeastern Jordan are enough to supply the nation's natural gas consumption.

MINING AND MANUFACTURING

Jordan's industrial output contributes 28.7 percent (2005 estimate) of its GDP. Its industrial base primarily consists of small factories, few of which employ high-technology methods. Heavy industries are either part of the public sector or are heavily supported by the government. Mining provides the largest single share of the country's domestic economy. This is mostly phosphate and potash from the Dead Sea. Salt, limestone (used in making cement), gypsum, and marble are also mined. The country's

Opposite: **A Jordanian woman buys small sticks from a street vendor in a bustling market in Amman. These soft, small sticks have been used for cleaning teeth since the time of Prophet Muhammad.**

major industries for domestic production are paper and cardboard (using imported wood chips), detergents, phosphates, alcoholic drinks, and petroleum refining. There are industrial courts to handle trade disputes.

Jordan's main export partners in 2005 were the United States (29.3 percent), Iraq (15.5 percent), India (8.5 percent), and Saudi Arabia (5.9 percent). Its main import partners were Saudi Arabia (21.1 percent), China (8.1 percent), Germany (7.2 percent), and the United States (6.3 percent). Its main exports are clothing, phosphates, fertilizer, potash, vegetables, manufactured goods, and pharmaceuticals. Its main imports are crude oil, fabrics, machinery, transportation equipment, and various manufactured goods.

AGRICULTURE

Less than 10 percent of Jordan's land is arable. Because of this, agriculture accounts for only a small part of its economy and its exports—about 3.5 percent of its GDP in 2005. The main products are wheat, barley, corn, millet, lentils, beans, peas, sesame, tobacco, tomatoes, cucumbers, citrus fruits (mostly lemons), melons, cabbages, potatoes, onions, and bananas. Modern methods have greatly increased productivity, and most of the vegetables are exported.

Although the most common farm animals are sheep, goats, and chickens, the latter is the only livestock the country can produce enough of to satisfy domestic demand; it produces less than 30 percent of its beef and lamb requirements. There is a small fishing industry from the Red Sea. Despite the popular image of camels in Arabian deserts, the few camels in Jordan are found only mostly among the Bedouins and in the Camel Corps. The most common work animals are donkeys and horses.

Forestation is a high priority of the government; seedlings are provided to farmers free of charge. The only natural forests are those on some hills of the Jordan River Valley and in some areas on the high plateau.

TOURISM

When the West Bank was part of Jordan, tourism was the country's largest single source of income. Jordan lost that income with the 1967 loss of the West Bank and its main tourist attraction, the ancient and holy city of Jerusalem. Nevertheless, Jordan receives about 2 million tourists annually, contributing as much as 10 percent of its GDP and more foreign exchange than all the country's exports combined. In 2003 the Ministry of Tourism and Antiquities formed the National Tourism Council, a joint government-private group that is working to increase tourism dramatically by 2010. Jordan has the highest proportion of Western tourists of any Arab country except Egypt.

The ruins of former civilizations (particularly Petra); the stark, pristine beauty of the desert; and the coastal resort area of Aqaba are likely to help draw larger numbers of visitors in the future. Moreover, Jordan's being home to many important religious sites of both Christianity and Islam should further enhance its tourism sector.

The scenic seaside feel of the Aqaba coast makes Jordan a great haven for tourism.

JOBS

About 82.5 percent of Jordan's labor force works in the services sector, for both government and private sectors. Another 12.5 percent works in mining and manufacturing. That includes factories involved in milling, brewing, oil pressing, canning, and furniture making, as well as in pharmaceutical and cement production. Only a scant 5 percent work in agriculture. Additionally, an estimated 300,000 Jordanians work abroad, and many of these remit a part of their income to families remaining behind.

Although wages are low by Western standards, so are prices. If we were to compare the wages of an average middle-aged bank worker in

Jordan with one in Syria, for example, taking into account differences in the prices of goods and services in these two countries, findings reveal that the worker in Syria has a buying power of around $100 a month, while the worker in Jordan has a buying power of a little over $400 a month, according to figures released by the World Bank in 2003.

For example, a car in Syria is beyond the wildest dreams of a bank worker—a 10-year-old economy model costs more than $10,000—while a car of the same model and age in Jordan costs only $2,000 to $3,000. A Syrian looking for a new apartment in Damascus will have to fork out $100,000 or more for a very modest place, while the Jordanian can buy a similar home in Amman for less than half that amount.

Professional jobs may be harder to come by, but life goes on in the thriving marketplace as it has for centuries.

Some things in Jordan do cost more, however. If these two workers stop on the street to buy a *shawarma* (shah-WAHR-mah), a meat or poultry burrito-type sandwich, the Syrian will pay about 50 cents, but the Jordanian will pay just less than a dollar.

Jordan's population is one of the best educated in the Arab world, and most people work in white-collar jobs. Foreign laborers, some of whom are in the country illegally, hold many of the lower-paying jobs. Many of these foreigners now work in Jordan's export factories, of which 90 percent are foreign-owned. As of 2001, Jordan had 17 trade unions in its General Federation of Trade Unions to handle trade disputes.

ECONOMIC PROBLEMS

Jordan has many economic difficulties. In 2005 total exports stood at $4.23 billion, while imports cost $8.68 billion—and there has always been a similar trade deficit. In 1991 foreign debt stood at $1.6 billion; in 2005 the figure was $8.27 billion.

The economy has to support nearly a million Palestinian and Iraqi refugees, even though, to a certain degree, the UNRWA (United Nations Relief and Works Agency) deals with most services provided to the Palestinian victims of war.

Annual population growth is estimated at 2.5 percent (2005), with less than 40 percent of the population under 14 years of age (2006). The unemployment rate was 8 percent in 1986, increased to 19 percent by 1991, and now stands at about 12.5 percent officially, but unofficial estimates climb as high as 30 percent.

Old and new modes of transportation make a striking contrast.

TRANSPORTATION

As of 2003 Jordan had about 4,565 miles (7,347 km) of paved roads. Two routes south of Amman lead to Aqaba: the Desert Highway and the King's Highway. The Allenby Bridge is the main crossing point over the Jordan River for those traveling to the West Bank. The original Hejaz Railway built by the Ottomans has been rebuilt and expanded. The port in Aqaba is small but handles several million tons of goods annually. It is the terminus of an oil pipeline for Iraqi oil. A recently built highway to Iraq from Aqaba shortens that trip.

The country's only airline, Royal Jordanian Air (Alia), is profitable and one of the best in the Mediterranean basin. It serves Jordan out of the single international airport outside Amman; there is also a small airport in Aqaba. The national bus service, JETT, is inexpensive, efficient, and makes several runs daily to Damascus in Syria, about 200 miles (320 km) from Amman. The most common taxi vehicle is the Mercedes Benz.

ENVIRONMENT

JORDAN HAS ESSENTIALLY THE same environmental problems as the other desert countries of North Africa and the Middle East. The main problems are, of course, the lack of water and the poor quality of what little there is. There are also other environmental issues.

WATER POLLUTION

There are two types of water pollution: chemical (such as from factories) and microbial (from untreated sewage). Urban areas have sewage treatment plants, but some parts of Jordan either have inadequate or no sewage treatment at all. As a result, surface water is mostly contaminated, and dysentery as well as chemical poisoning is common, especially in summer when surface water is low and pollutants are more concentrated. Industrial wastewater contamination is particularly bad in Zarqa, the main industrial center of the country. Where mining is done near bodies of water, rainwater that seeps through mine tailings residue gradually pollutes surface water. Also, chemicals associated with mining can leach into groundwater.

Amman's water supply is often plagued by foul-smelling algae that threaten to make the water undrinkable. The algae develop because of the intensity of the sun's rays on the still body of water in its reservoir. In 1998 the minister of water affairs was forced to resign because the problem became so critical. Children and the elderly are the most seriously affected by this situation. The government has released thousands of algae-eating fish into the reservoir to try to clean it up.

Above: **Treated sewage effluent, which will irrigate surrounding farmlands, flows freely into a ditch.**

Opposite: **A river foaming with detergent and waste. Jordan's lack of clean drinking water is exacerbated by the fact that the country shares much of its water source with its neighbors.**

Finally, the Gulf of Aqaba, a prime tourist area with spectacular marine life, is becoming dirtier because of the dumping of oil and other petroleum products by the many ships that come into Jordan's only port, and also due to pollutants released from factories in the area, most notably chemical fertilizer plants.

AIR POLLUTION

The production of potash, phosphate, and cement makes up a big chunk of the Jordanian economy and its exports. These products, of course, all require mining. Powdered dust rising from mining activities and mine tailings can pollute the air and waters. Most of these mining residues also contain such toxins as fluorine gas, sulfur dioxide, carbon dioxide, and radiation.

While Jordan has little heavy industry compared with most of the world's biggest economies, it is unable, like most developing countries, to strictly regulate the emissions from what little industry it does have. Most developing countries have to deal with problems of inadequate infrastructure, international debt, and often underpaid (and therefore easily bribed) enforcement officials. Jordan is no exception, and the government is probably more concerned about feeding its population and sustaining its economy than about the "luxury" of environmental protection.

The most serious industrial pollution comes from the cement plants in Fuheis (a large suburb west of Amman), the oil refineries and power generating plants in Zarqa, the battery factories surrounding the capital, and the port and industrial activities in Aqaba.

Related to this issue, Arab society has an interesting concept that is not foreign to most Western cultures: what we call "bribery" has a parallel in the Arabic language, *rushweh* (roosh-WAYH), which is used

for serious offenses. The word "baksheesh," however, means something more like "tip," and is used for less severe cases. Both cause problems in maintaining the law. For example, a policeman there who stops a traffic offender may be offered a tip to let the offender go; a worker in a government office might speed up the process of, perhaps, issuing a visa by several days if he is paid baksheesh. If a government inspector finds unacceptable situations in a factory, he is more likely to accept a tip and be lenient than to insist on compliance. More importantly, related to the issue of environmental problems, people who posses *wasta* (WAHS-ta), which means having contacts in the right places, often if not always get off the hook for their destroying the environment by evading laws of environmental conservation and preservation.

In summer, the main sources of air pollution in Jordan are motor vehicles. Of the approximately 300,000 registered vehicles in Jordan, about 200,000 are in Amman. Additionally, most of them use leaded gasoline or high-sulfur (low-quality) diesel fuel. There is a Ministry of Environment and a branch of the traffic police that inspects vehicles, though not always

Zarqa is the center of Jordan's heavy industries. They involve a very high output of smoke, causing the air to be extremely unclean.

Female traffic police officers directing traffic in central Amman. Growing urbanization has inevitably led to an increasing number of vehicles on Jordan's roads and higher levels of air pollutants in the country's atmosphere.

effectively. But again, the problem is not the lack of agency but the lack of assertiveness among the authorities to enforce the laws pertaining to environmental issues. Indeed, since there is a large number of poor people in the populace who cannot afford new cars, most personal vehicles are very old U.S. cars made before environmental controls. Trucks, too, are often ancient models that pump out emissions that would put them off the road for good in most Western countries. Most vehicles also lack mufflers and catalytic converters. Thus, noise pollution is rampant and the city air is often very polluted.

In winter, air pollution can be worse at times, as millions of Jordanians heat their homes with kerosene. Many of the stoves and furnaces used are also old and woefully inefficient, emitting large quantities of partially burned hydrocarbons.

WASTE DISPOSAL

Garbage collection systems are fairly good in urban centers but not in small towns and rural areas, if they exist there at all. Solid waste is not separated, however, and often includes hazardous substances. In fact, some estimates claim there are now more than 13,000 tons of hazardous waste scattered around the country.

LAND DEGRADATION

The degeneration of land to desert (desertification) in Jordan is a very valid environmental concern. The degradation of the land has been the result of unregulated urban expansion, overgrazing, inefficient irrigation, deforestation, and mining. Of course, all of these factors are exacerbated by the constant and rapid population growth of the country. In a land that is mostly uninhabitable desert, the increasing population pressure heavily taxes the small percentage of land that gets enough rainfall or otherwise has water resources just enough to support the people and domestic animals that live on it.

The enchanting moonlike landscape and desert terrain of the Wadi Rum Nature Reserve host many species of rare plants.

ENDANGERED SPECIES

According to the Jordanian Royal Society for the Conservation of Nature (the first Arab environmental organization), research shows that, in Jordan, between 200 and 250 species are considered rare and 100 to 150 species are threatened. Among animal species considered threatened are about 46 mammals, 11 birds, four reptiles, six freshwater fish, two marine invertebrates, and four marine vertebrates. One of the endangered mammals is the magnificent Arabian oryx, which was reintroduced several years ago (with no small effort) after having become extinct in the wild.

EFFORTS TO SOLVE THE PROBLEMS

The most arduous efforts seem to target the country's biggest challenge—meeting its water needs. For example, in 2000 a new education program was established that aims to change people's behavior in relation to the use of water. Water Efficiency and Public Information for Action (WEPIA) is a joint effort by the Jordanian Ministry of Water and Irrigation and the American Academy for Educational Development. A representative of the Academy states the goal of the group succinctly: "We don't like the word 'awareness.' It is not enough. Many people are aware of the situation,

Increasing desertification and the growing scarcity of water are pressing environmental concerns that Jordan has to grapple with.

but what are they doing about it? WEPIA wants to create more than awareness. We want to change attitudes and behavioral patterns. People's use of the resource has to change fundamentally and lastingly."

The organization sponsors major media campaigns and designs educational programs at all education levels. Perhaps most significant, though, is its hands-on approach in distributing water-saving devices for homes and institutions as well as auditing water consumption and implementing the use of such devices at hospitals, universities, and businesses.

The government also introduced a water reuse program in which irrigation and other types of water are recycled and reused. This program cannot realize its full potential, however, without supporting infrastructure such as reusing/recycling systems in apartment buildings. The government has enlisted the assistance of North American university specialists to help solve its perennial problem of algae contamination of Amman's drinking water reserve.

In addition to the government's efforts, several nongovernmental organizations (NGOs) are trying to help. The Royal Society for the Conservation of Nature (RSCN), begun in 1996 by Queen Noor, monitors endangered and threatened species as well as pollution problems. It has set up more than 1,000 Nature Conservation Clubs in schools, trying to educate young people in order to change their attitudes and lifestyles, while also running four of the country's nature reserves. Another group is Friends of the Earth Middle East, a group of Israeli, Jordanian, and Palestinian environmentalists who strive to push through corrective legislation and educate the public. Established in l996, the group also produces many environmental publications related to specific issues in the region.

In 1992 the World Conservation Union (IUCN) assisted a group of more than 180 Jordanian specialists from different areas of society in completing a comprehensive working paper called "National Environment Strategy for Jordan." The paper gives over 400 specific recommendations regarding a wide variety of issues relating to both the environment and economic development.

Another interesting project, started in the late 1990s, is funded by the United Nations Development Program, along with the Danish and Jordanian governments. It will use one of the biggest landfills in the country to produce electricity by burning methane gas. Additionally, the solid waste from the dump can be rendered into fertilizer for agricultural use.

A Jordanian girl plays on a swing in one of the many public parks in the country during World Environment Day in Amman.

JORDANIANS

JORDAN HAS THE MOST HOMOGENEOUS POPULATION of any Arab country, both ethnically and religiously. For example, the percentages of Muslims in Jordan, Syria, and Lebanon are about 97 percent, 90 percent, and 60 percent, respectively. All but a handful of Jordan's population is Arab, and the primary difference is between urban and rural, Palestinian and Bedouin. Usually Palestinian-Jordanians are the urban residents, while the rural people are Bedouins or their descendents.

POPULATION STATISTICS

Like all Arab countries, Jordan has suffered a population explosion since World War II (WWII). Its annual growth rate has been almost 4 percent over the past three decades, although since the late 1990s that has dropped to about 2.5 percent. A big part of this growth is the result of high birthrates, but refugees from both Palestine and Iraq have contributed greatly at certain times. In fact, people of Palestinian origin account for some 60 percent of Jordan's population.

Just before Jordan became a country in 1921, the population was 230,000. In 1938 the estimated population was 300,000—many of them Palestinians fleeing violence in Palestine. In 1952 there were 680,000 people in the country, nearly half of them Palestinians expelled from the new Jewish country of Israel. In 1979 the population reached 2.1 million. In 1990 there were 3.2 million residents; only a year later the population had swollen to 4.1 million, due in part to an inflow of Iraqi refugees from the Gulf War and Jordanian workers returning from Iraq and Kuwait.

The second war in Iraq has further increased the numbers of both refugees and permanent residents. For example, according to the Statistical Yearbook 2003 of the United Nations High Commission for Refugees, there were nearly 1,000 Iraqi refugees in the country plus more than 3,300 others

Opposite: **A group of young Jordanian teenage girls at the Roman theater in Amman.**

who were applying for asylum. According to the 2003 census, Jordan's population was 5,460,000; but a 2006 estimate puts the population at a little over 5.9 million. In spite of differing ideologies between the various groups of people, the government has sought to promote a sense of national identity.

RACE AND CLASS

Palestinians are generally better educated and more Westernized in social characteristics than other Arabs, making them a bit more egalitarian. Since the majority of Jordanians are Palestinian, the country has less obvious racism than many other Arab countries. Class-consciousness, however, is common. No matter how much wealth one has, it is how one shows it that counts. There is very little socializing between the upper and lower classes, and educated city dwellers tend to feel superior toward illiterate villagers and the Bedouins.

Manual labor of any kind is thought to be beneath the dignity of anyone in the upper classes. The majority of wealthy Jordanians, for example, must employ foreign servants to do the household chores as well as to take care of their children. To some wealthy Jordanians, Arabs from poorer countries such as Yemen and Egypt are considered inferior. They may also scorn what they view as the archaic tribalism and crude customs of the Bedouins.

DRESS

Most Jordanians dress in Western fashions. Generally, only the Bedouins and some villagers wear more traditional garb such as the *kaffiyeh* and various other garments. At night and in colder weather, a heavy sleeveless coat may be worn.

COMMON JORDANIAN CHARACTERISTICS

- Almost all men smoke.
- Few keep pets.
- People (especially men) drive very fast.
- Most Jordanians do not like to exercise.
- There is little violent crime in Jordan.
- Most men do not wear silk, diamonds, or gold; these are thought to be for women only.
- Most women do not use veils, but many wear head scarves instead.
- Men carry strings of prayer beads, often rolling the beads (made from stone, bone, or ceramic) between their fingers. Each string has 33 beads—the number of names used for God.
- In Muslim courts, mothers are invariably given priority in custodianship or control of their children in settlements of divorce.

Many women follow Muslim tradition by wearing head scarves and full-length, long-sleeved dresses, but these have a modern look with bright colors and snug fits. In some communities, such as country villages and Palestinian refugee camps, the women take great pride in their embroidery skills, displayed on their everyday clothes. Girls learn such needlecrafts from an early age.

Middle- and upper-class women like bright colors, elaborate designs, lots of jewelry and makeup, high-heeled shoes, and long hair that is heavily coifed. Blue jeans, T-shirts, running shoes, and other such casual dress are also common, especially among teenagers. Young men of the middle and upper classes usually wear their hair short and are very dressy. They tend to be brand conscious, coveting American and European labels.

Few Jordanians—only very Westernized youths—wear shorts, miniskirts, short hair (for women or girls), or long hair (for men). Others are often torn between their cultural heritage and influences from the West. Many younger adults, however, are beginning to develop an appreciation for their ancestors' traditional dress and wear them on special occasions. Devout Muslim women rarely expose more than their hands, ankles, and, sometimes, face.

MINORITY GROUPS

More than half the population is Palestinian, while descendants of the traditional Bedouins make up most of the rest. There are a few minority groups in Jordan.

PALESTINIANS It seems illogical to categorize these as a minority when Palestinians are the majority in the country. But there is a distinction between those who have integrated into Jordanian society, have become economically successful, and hold no hope of returning to their former homeland—nor do they desire to return—and other Palestinians who live in refugee camps and are usually first generation refugees and their children. Both the settled Palestinians and the refugees enjoy full Jordanian citizenship, but the latter are termed "refugees" primarily to qualify them for assistance—medical, economic, and social—from the

Bedouin men sitting on the ground in a circle, drinking coffee and talking about the day's events.

United Nations Refugee and Works Agency (UNRWA). While there is no racial difference between the two, the integrated, successful Palestinians often feel superior to the refugees.

BEDOUINS It is ironic that the Bedouins, who were the only inhabitants of Jordan's land outside the East Bank just a few generations ago, are now a minority group. They can be distinguished from other Arabs by their shorter, thinner bodies, smaller and pointed facial features; and their generally darker skin tones.

Their Arabic name, Badoo (BAH-doo), means "desert dweller" and comes from the same Arabic root word as *badiya* (BAH-dee-yah), which means "desert" or "steppe." They are traditionally a nomadic people, and before the advent of modernization, camels were their main means of transportation. Without camels the Bedouins would have found it difficult to survive in the desert. The camel is ideally suited because it can store enough water and fat in its hump to last up to several days. The largest Bedouin groups are the Bani Sukhurs, Huwayatats, and Sirhans.

Despite the erosion of the Bedouins' traditional lifestyle, many elements of their culture live on in the daily lives of most Jordanians: segregation of genders, arranged marriages, loyalty to clan, submission to a strong and autocratic leader, belief in harsh punishments, an unsparing code of honor, and warm hospitality.

Mealtime for children in a Palestinian refugee camp.

REFUGEES The two wars in Iraq are also contributing to changes in the face of Jordan's population. There is an official Iraqi refugee camp at

Ruweished, only a short distance from the Iraqi border, where several hundred refugees from the most recent war in Iraq stay. The Jordanian government officially stated that there were about 300,000 Iraqis currently in Jordan. The Interior Ministry claims that these outsiders are there on business or vacation and so are not refugees, while the United Nations High Commission for Refugees (UNHCR) holds that only 800 Iraqis have received official refugee status and some 15,000 others are under temporary protection as asylum seekers. Street estimates in Amman for such Iraqi refugees are around 500,000 people.

CIRCASSIANS AND CHECHENS In the 1880s, the Russian czar sent troops to invade the small central-Asian area now called Chechnya in a

A GOAT-HAIR HOUSE

Only 1 percent of Jordan's population now lives in tents, but a romantic image still lingers in the hearts of many Arabs of the strong and independent nomad, and the goat-hair tent invokes a visual demonstration of Arabian nights and romance.

Goat's wool is woven outdoors, on looms, into strips of cloth 24–32 inches (60–80 cm) wide by Bedouin women. Six to eight of these strips are then sewn together, making each tent between 12 and 15 feet (3.7 and 4.6 m) wide. The length of tents may vary, but the width remains the same. Center poles 10–13 feet (3–4 m) apart divide tents into "rooms" with the help of woven "walls" 3–5 feet (1–1.5 m) high. Most tents have two such rooms: one where the women sleep and the other for the men. Extended families may have three, with the extra room for a son's family. Only sheikhs (tribal leaders) have tents with four to five rooms, since great hospitality is expected of them when people come to visit.

Living in a tent that is larger than what a family actually needs is considered pretentious and also increases the expectation for hospitality because tent size proclaims wealth and position. The interiors of most village houses are designed like those of the tents.

form of crusade against the Muslims there. In order to save some of their fellow believers, the Ottomans resettled several thousand Circassians and Chechens—two separate tribes—in Transjordan.

The Circassians were relocated in the area of Amman. They rebuilt the city, established the manufacturing city of Zarqa, and introduced large-wheeled carts and a system of dirt roads in the Amman-Zarqa area. Their descendants now have a sizeable presence in the country. The Circassians, with their industrious character, also set up an economic pattern that continues today. This group is well-integrated into society, with high government and business positions, although socially they maintain a certain distance from the Arabs. There are about 25,000 of them today, and they have their own language and culture.

Circassian children perform to mark the end of the school year.

The Chechens also have their own language and culture but have not been as economically successful as the Circassians. Except for a few Iraqi refugees, they are the only Shi'ite Muslims in Jordan, and their current population numbers only about 2,500.

CHRISTIANS This group is a minority only in respect to religion: they are all Arabs and bear most of the same cultural characteristics of the general population. The Christians have never been persecuted in Jordan and are, in fact, allies of the government, not opponents. They hold many positions in government, education, and business and—like the Circassians—are among the most prosperous and best-educated citizens. While only a decade or so ago they constituted about 6 percent of the population, that

THE POWER OF LEGENDS

In traditional Arab culture, legends dramatized the standards to be lived up to. Here is the story of Hatim at-Tay, relating to Arab hospitality.

Before his birth, Hatim's mother had a dream in which she had the choice of having 10 sons as brave as eagles, or only one who would surpass all men in generosity. She chose the latter. One day, as a youth, Hatim was sent to pasture the family's camels. He returned soon after, happily saying that he had brought fame to his ancestral name by giving away all the camels as gifts.

Hatim's generosity continued through his long life and did not end with his death. Years later, a rival tribe that was jealous of his reputation was camping near his grave and scorning his deeds. During the night Hatim appeared in a dream to the leader of the group, inviting the man to feast on his tribe's only camel. In the morning the man discovered that his camel was dead, so the tribe did feast on it.

As the people went on their way after breakfast, they met Hatim's son leading a black camel. He told the tribe that his father had appeared in a dream the night before and ordered him to find the tribe traveling without a camel so that he could give it the black one.

proportion has declined to 3 to 4 percent. The lower birthrate among Christians versus the higher birthrate among Muslims, coupled with the inflow of Muslim refugees, is the reason for the change.

Most Christians belong to the Eastern Orthodox and Greek Catholic churches, but there are some Roman Catholics and Protestants as well. They trace the roots of their religion back to the pre-Islamic era when Christianity was founded in the region and was later upheld by the Roman rulers. Near the border with Syria there remains a very small group of Samaritans who are descendants of an ancient Jewish sect.

ATTITUDE TOWARD FOREIGNERS

While hospitality is the norm among all Arabs, educated city dwellers seem to have lost much of the overwhelming hospitality that is still so common among the Bedouins and villagers. A small shopkeeper, however, will serve tea or coffee to anyone who comes by, and most people will also be helpful when a visitor has any sort of problem. Willingness to give assistance to a needy outsider is deeply ingrained in Arab consciousness.

In the desert and villages it is still common for travelers to be invited into a Bedouin tent or a village house for tea or coffee. Many questions will be asked of the visitor, as most people, especially the children, are very curious about foreigners. Despite the general friendliness, there are some characteristics of Jordanian culture that may disturb outsiders.

STARING In Arab culture it is not rude for one man to stare at another, as it would be in the United States, for example. However, it is a norm among Jordanians not to stare at each other when passing in the street unless they are acquaintances. It is considered rude for men to stare intensely at a woman; however, it is constantly being done, even if she is with another man. To foreigners, the intensity and duration of the stare is often most unsettling, but if the foreigner stares back, the Arab will not be embarrassed and may actually strike up a conversation with the visitor. The greatest interest is directed toward light-haired, fair-skinned people.

A Bedouin encampment in the Wadi Rum. Some camps have special tents for guests, and it is customary to prepare lavish feasts for them.

LACK OF PERSONAL SPACE In Arab culture there is a different concept of personal public space, as the Arabs' need for privacy differs from that of the Western world. Westerners feel the lack of personal space. For example, when people are in public in Jordan, they can expect to get jostled, and this applies to foreigners as well. There are, however, many unwritten rules that guarantee women private space from men in public, and it even extends to the behavior of men actually giving their seats to women so they won't be jostled on a crowded bus. Even so, bumping into another person is not considered rude and apologies are

Thousands of foreigners visit Wadi Rum every year to take in its picturesque desert beauty and to hike and trek on its terrain.

"Hospitality is a byword among Arabs, whatever their station in life. ... When they say, as they often do, 'My home is your home,' they mean it."

—*Margaret K. Nydell, Arabist scholar*

seldom offered. It is this mix of attitudes toward social etiquette that may make a foreigner feel very conflicted about the Jordanian perception of personal space.

PERSONAL QUESTIONS Many Jordanians are curious about foreigners and ask them personal questions, much as they do among themselves. For example: "How much did your car cost?" "How much do you pay for rent?" "Are you married?" "Why aren't you married?" They do not understand if a visitor is reluctant to answer some of the questions, particularly with regard to marital status and financial matters.

CHANGING ATTITUDES This is most marked among rural people. The changes are seen in many aspects of their daily life. Even the nomadic Bedouins are finding it difficult to move from place to place as they are accumulating more possessions and modern conveniences. For example,

Jordanians shopping for fresh produce in a market in Amman.

one can see some goat-hair tents with Japanese-made trucks parked beside them and gasoline generators running outside the tent to provide electricity. As a result, families put off changing campsites for as long as they can.

Another change is that fewer camels are kept nowadays, as alternative modes of transportation are available. Many camel herders have turned to keeping sheep, which are easier to tend. Today not all nomads are whole families on the move. Many are just individuals who are hired to look after camels or sheep belonging to others.

In addition to this, many Bedouins have adopted a more urban lifestyle out of economic needs, as not much income can be attained simply from shepherding these days. The life of the Bedouin shepherd is fast becoming replaced by blue- and white-collar professionals as more and more are acquiring education and training in specific fields of interest. For example, many Bedouins have become tour guides, businessmen, and teachers.

LIFESTYLE

THE LIFESTYLE OF JORDAN'S WEALTHY, college-educated city dwellers is different from that of the less-educated rural people. They all share a love for socializing, however. The rhythm of Jordanian life is set by the call to prayer five times a day. Though not as many stick to it as rigidly as they once did, the day's flow remains the same: the late start in the morning to the day's activities (generally around 9 or 10 A.M.), the midafternoon lunch and extended rest period while the intense heat of midday passes (usually from 1 P.M. to 4 or 5 P.M.), and late nights. Most shops stay open until 9 or 10 P.M., and Jordanians do not eat dinner until after 8 P.M. It is a very typical Mediterranean lifestyle, not a lot different from that of Italy or coastal Spain.

Above: **Even the Bedouins have adapted to some "foreign" ways, and shaking hands is now common, sometimes replacing the traditional embrace.**

Opposite: **Two Bedouin men and their trusted camels in Wadi Rum Desert.**

Wealthy Jordanians travel a lot, and most have been to North America and Europe. They also have relatives who live in these places. In Jordan, they may live in what Americans would call luxury condominiums, which often take up a whole floor of a large condo building; some live in single-family villas, while others have these as second homes. They drive expensive new cars; hire domestics to clean, cook, and help raise their children; and wear the latest Western fashions. The wealthy urban Palestinians, in particular, seem to like all things Western.

SOCIALIZING

A traveler who visits Jordan for the first time will notice the energy the residents put into personal relationships. It is obvious on the streets and in homes, schools, and offices. Friends greet each other emotionally, with

Jordanians are comfortable with just being part of the hustle and bustle of life. No one likes to stand out too much in a crowd.

both parties talking at the same time. They ask about each other's families, work or studies, and health, and always extend an invitation to the other party to visit them at home and have tea or coffee. Then they say good-bye in several ways, always bestowing blessings on each other.

PHYSICAL CLOSENESS Part of Arab social intensity is shown by physical closeness: male friends hug and kiss each other and women do the same. Jordanian friends of the same gender touch each other frequently. Young lovers and older married people sometimes walk arm-in-arm or holding hands, but there is rarely any public emotional display between opposite genders. Few men and women or boys and girls are just friends, not only because of the usual segregation that is inherent in Arab and Islamic culture, but also because even the concept is foreign to most of them. If you are a man, your friends are men; if you are a woman, your friends are women.

CULTURAL ATTITUDES

Most Jordanians love to laugh, joke, eat, and talk. They also like loud music, car horns, loud voices, and hand clapping. Although Amman is much quieter than Damascus or Cairo, it is quite noisy in the crowded areas of the city where the poorer classes live. As families become better off, children are less involved in the workforce and can enjoy the pleasures of childhood. Arabs, whether Christian or Muslim, strongly

A Jordanian family shops at a street market.

believe in fate, and that belief shows in their constant use of the word *insha'allah* (in-SHAH-ahl-LAH), meaning "God willing," whenever they talk about the future. This "culture of fate" shows up in other ways as well. For example, they are not particularly concerned about punctuality and schedules. Being on time does not matter, because whatever is going to happen will happen anyway.

GROUP CONFORMITY Being part of a clan is ingrained in Arab tradition. The immediate family commands first loyalty, then clan or village (sometimes these are the same), ethnic group, religion, and finally, nationality. King Hussein himself once said, "We are Arabs first and Jordanians second."

There seems to be a certain lack of individuality among Jordanians, for they do not like to stand out too much from the group. This is because family interests take precedence over those of the individual. Truly original artists and writers, for example, are rare, and the naming of children is tradition-bound. Literally half the Jordanian males are named Muhammad or Mohammed (moo-HAHM-muhd). Many use their middle names for a

Jordanians enjoy a slow, easy, and carefree social life where playing games and socializing is more important than the comings and goings of the modern world.

75

little distinction. Other popular names include Ahmad (AH-muhd), Khalil (kha-LEEL), Khaled (KHA-led), Yassar (yahs-SAR), Imad (ai-MUHD), and Samer (SAH-mer). There is only a slightly larger choice of women's names. Because of all this, some modern Arabic scholars lament their people's devotion to tradition at the expense of innovative and creative thinking.

GENDER SEPARATION Gender segregation and the social and familial taboos on dating create sexual naiveté. When they are in the presence of women, men in their 20s or even early 30s often behave like adolescents. The concept of gender separation is so deeply ingrained that in many traditional

An Arab man with a young wife. Muslim men are traditionally allowed to have up to four wives.

families, women do not dine with the men if there are guests from outside the family present at the meal.

IMPORTANCE OF THE FAMILY

Families are the main focus of Jordanian life, and children are so important (especially sons) that fathers and mothers assume nicknames after the first child is born. For example, if the son is named Mahmoun, the father becomes known as Abu Mahmoun (literally, father of Mahmoun) and the mother becomes Umm Mahmoun (mother of Mahmoun). If no sons are born, the mother usually identifies herself as the mother of the first-born daughter; fathers rarely do this, however. Most Arabs feel that being without children and family is very tragic, and Jordanians are no exception to this.

MARRIAGES

Finding a marriage partner is a preoccupation for most Jordanians beyond their midteens. Arranged marriages are still the norm in villages and among the Bedouins. Even modern city people often cannot marry just anyone they please; both families usually have to consent to the union. First cousins still marry each other and are considered the best match. It is also quite common for the mother of a young woman to approach a young man she would like to see her daughter marry and ask if he is interested in marriage. Divorces are rare, and since marriage is the main goal in life, wedding parties are major social events, sometimes lasting for several days, although with the men and women celebrating separately.

"The Islamic system is not so much opposed to the woman as to the male-female relation itself.... Such relation, if developed into an encompassing love involvement satisfying the physical, emotional, and intellectual needs of both partners, is considered as a detraction from the male's full allegiance to God."

—Issa J. Boullata, Arabist scholar

HOMEMADE WEDDING DRESSES

Bedouins and villagers are traditional people. One custom they practiced was for a young woman to create her own wedding dress—with considerable help from older, experienced women. The patterns of the dresses were set by the village or clan tradition, although there were personal variations within those patterns. Traditional gowns were usually black and always had extensive, elaborate embroidery in unique patterns and bright colors. A dress took a year or longer to sew by hand and was often "signed" by the maker: her name was embroidered onto some part of the garment. The left side of the dress was often highly decorated, while the right side had only coarse, simple designs; this is because a baby is traditionally carried on the right arm—the dresses were also worn long after the wedding. Today, most wedding dresses are made by the local tailor.

For tourists, such gowns are purchases prized for their intricate beauty and the tremendous amount of work that has gone into them.

DEATHS

In Islam, burials cannot take place after sunset, and the body needs to be buried within a full day following death. Bodies are first washed (a man by his wife, or mother if he is unmarried; a woman usually by other women). This is a religious and social ritual during which special words are spoken for each part of the body. Muslims are not allowed to be embalmed or cremated when they die, so they must be buried within hours, without clothes and wrapped in a shroud.

During the three days of mourning, friends, relatives, and neighbors visit the family. In Muslim village homes, the family is expected to feed all guests, whereas in the cities, the guests usually come and go informally, without causing much of a need for food preparation on the part of the grieving family. Women relatives wear black for many months after a death. In due time, they can start wearing a combination of black and white. In very traditional families, it may be a year or longer before the women can wear other colors again. Even in more modern families, this time is usually at least several months. If an older woman's husband dies and she does not remarry, she may wear black for the rest of her life. These traditions are similar in both Eastern Orthodox and Muslim families, although the wealthier, college-educated Palestinians usually do not adhere to such traditions nowadays. In traditional circles, however, a woman who does not fulfill the mourning traditions is harshly criticized.

WOMEN'S ROLES

Women who stay single into their late 20s or beyond stand little chance of marrying anyone except perhaps a much older widower, a divorced man, or one who already has a wife but wants a younger one. Such a woman is considered to be deficient in some way and will invariably

continue living with her family, taking care of her aging parents. Although women are not prevented by civil law from living alone or with another woman as a roommate, they are discouraged from doing so by powerful social and family pressures.

Despite these traditional attitudes, the royal family and others in Jordanian society are fighting hard to make the life of women better. More women than men are now enrolled in Jordan's education system (76 percent in 2002); yet, according to the World Bank, women make up only from 12 to 25 percent of the workforce. Female literacy has increased from 29 percent in 1970 to 70 percent in 1990 and to more than 86 percent in 2003 (compared with about 96 percent for males in the same year), yet the percentage of women in the workforce has barely increased at all. Two-thirds of working women are in government jobs, half of them as teachers. About 15 percent work in banking.

Women can also run for political office and hold any government position. In 1993 three women ran for the lower house of parliament, the House of

In a male-dominated society such as that in Muslim countries, women are traditionally expected to tend the home and look after the children.

79

The modernization of Jordanian women is very much on the agenda of the government, yet stereotypical roles between men and women are hard to change even now.

Representatives, and one of them, Toujan Feisal, became the first woman to be so elected. Also, there are now 17 women judges (3.6 percent of the total), 7 women out of 55 members of the Senate, and 99 female members of various city councils. The proportion of women in senior administrative posts jumped from 4.6 percent in 1995 to 9.9 percent in 2002. Jordan now has one female ambassador, and nearly 23 percent of its diplomatic corps are women. In 1995 there were no women at the subministerial level of the government, but by 2002 there were 22. All these things indicate a slowly increasing female presence in higher places. Finally, women have had the right to inherit land since the 1930s, but family and social pressures often dictate otherwise. The biggest social fear is that the land will pass on to strangers (the woman's husband's family) upon her death.

It is hoped that the government's progressive attitude will continue to bring Jordanian women into the mainstream of society. The Queen Alia Fund and the Noor al-Hussein Foundation help create income-generating projects for women (especially in rural areas), and in the summer of 1993 a national conference of 500 men and women from all sectors of society created the National Women's Strategy. The strategy, which is concerned with the situation of women in legislation, economics, society, education, and health, has been formally endorsed by the government.

EDUCATION

Jordan's literacy rate in 1961 was only 32 percent, but it increased to 74 percent by 1987 and to about 91 percent in 2003 (females, 86.3 percent; males, 95.9 percent). Today most remaining illiterate people are the older Jordanians—especially those in the rural areas. In the early 1990s the Ministry of Education began reforming Jordan's education system, and this process was expedited in 2001 when King Abdullah II openly called for an overhaul of the system. Most of its problems are similar to those faced by other developing countries— lack of technology, absence of or poor quality of infrastructure, and high student-teacher ratios. In 2003 Jordan initiated the Education Reform for the Knowledge Economy initiative, a $380 million program to fulfill the king's mandate. The program is said to be the most ambitious of any country in the Middle East.

Jordan's Queen Rania speaks to schoolchildren at a primary school in a village in northern Jordan.

PRIMARY AND SECONDARY SCHOOLS

The Ministry of Education runs public schools, sets the curricula, and develops state examinations. Education is compulsory through the 10th grade. Beyond that point, there is a high dropout rate.

HIGHER EDUCATION Jordan has many universities; the eight major ones are Al al-Bayt, Amman, Mu'tah, Yarmouk, Zarka (private), the Hashemite University (in Zarqa and said to be the best in the land), King Hussein Bin Talal University (in Ma'an), and the University of Jordan. They are generally patterned after American universities and are often considered to be among the best institutions of higher education in the Arab world. They accept international students, most of whom come from other

Arab countries. There are also more than 50 technical and community colleges in addition to military institutes and a few missionary and international schools.

University students cannot study whatever they want, for the subjects that they are allowed to take during university are based upon their grades from the Tawjihi examination, which is usually taken in the last year of secondary school. Furthermore, the subjects taught at university are limited, although much less so than before 1990. From 1990 to 1998, university enrollment in Jordan climbed steadily, and while there were about 60,000 Jordanian students studying abroad in the mid-1980s, for example, only about 30,000 were doing so in 2000.

HEALTH CARE

The Ministry of Health was set up in 1950 to plan the development of the country's health-care service, which is high on the government's list of priorities. The cities of Amman, Zarqa, Irbid, and Aqaba have clean, well-equipped, modern private hospitals with well-trained doctors and nurses, and all villages have health clinics. Most of the doctors in Jordan speak English. A national health insurance program makes medical care affordable for all but the poorest citizens, and they can be treated at government clinics. Those clinics, though, have many serious problems such as overcrowding, understaffing, poorly trained personnel, and a scarcity of equipment. Additionally, the Jordan Human Development Report of 2004 states that, among the poorest people, inadequate nutrition causes much illness.

The only serious infectious disease that has not been brought under control is dysentery, and most cases arise from irrigation water's being contaminated by human waste. Perhaps the most serious health problem is heart disease caused by lack of exercise, heavy smoking, and high-fat diets. Life expectancy in Jordan is now 76 years for men—up from 63 years in the 1980s—and about 81 years for women—up from 67 years in the 1980s. The infant mortality rate is about 17 deaths per 1,000 live births, down dramatically from 54 deaths per 1,000 live births in the 1980s.

LIVING QUARTERS

Most residents of central Amman, Zarqa, and Irbid live in houses and apartments. Many of them own their places. Villagers live in simple cottages with one to three rooms. Almost all rural residents have electricity and running water, although many still do not have modern household appliances such as washing machines.

There is often a big difference between the interior furnishings and decorations of rural homes and those of wealthy, educated families in Amman. The rural homes have only functional furnishings that are both traditional and esthetic—handwoven carpets and handmade wooden furniture, for example—whereas those of the upper classes in the city are eclectic in appearance. Furniture, curtains, and lamps may be imported from Europe or North America, and they will generally be selected for their decorative value, as Jordanians love highly ornamental surroundings. Fabrics are usually brightly colored, frames are elaborately carved, and chandeliers are ostentatious. Persian and Turkish carpets, especially those made of silk, are popular.

The older, wealthy Jordanians have little desire to own the beautiful traditional handicrafts made in Jordan. Instead, they prefer things made in the United States or Europe, possibly because they are more expensive and conspicuous.

RELIGION

JORDANIANS—MUSLIMS AND CHRISTIANS ALIKE—share a strong belief in God. They thank God for everything and leave the future up to him. The most common response to "How are you?" is *"Al Hamdulla"* (ahl-HAHM-dool-lah), which means literally, "Thank Allah."

Today, around 94 percent of Jordan's people are Sunni Muslims (Sunni is the main branch of Islam), about 3 percent of the population is Christian, and about 3 percent of the people are Shi'a (also called Shiite) and Druze Muslims. The number of Shi'a Muslims in Jordan has increased significantly in recent years, partially due to the influx of refugees resulting from the two wars in Iraq. The country's constitution guarantees freedom of worship in all religions.

Above: **A Greek Orthodox Church in Bethany, Jordan. Christianity is one of the native religions in this country. Many of Jordan's inhabitants were Christian before the coming of Islam.**

Opposite: **The King Abdullah Mosque in Amman serves as a focal point of Islamic worship in Jordan.**

ANCIENT RELIGIONS

Before the eighth century, when the Muslim Omayyads swept across what is now Jordanian territory, many religions were practiced in the region. The Moabites, Edomites, Nabateans, Assyrians, Babylonians, Greeks, Romans, and Jews all tried to spread their own beliefs. After the death of Christ, however, most people in this land adhered to the monotheism (belief in one God) of Judaism and Christianity.

SUNNI ISLAM

The word "Islam" means "submission to Allah." Muslims believe this is not a new religion but a continuation of Judaism and Christianity, with

Muhammad being the last of the prophets and the Koran (also called "The Book") superseding all other revelations from God. In the Koran, Muslims, Jews, and Christians are all referred to as "children of The Book." Even though Judaism and Christianity are native to this part of the world, Islam quickly spread through the land with its beliefs.

THE STORY OF ISLAM

In A.D. 570 a boy named Muhammad was born into a noble Arab family in Mecca. As a youth, he was a shepherd. He also traveled with his uncle, learning of the world. He later married, had children, and became a successful merchant. He used to go to a certain cave to pray and meditate. Muslims believe that when he was about 40 years old he was visited in the cave by the angel Gabriel, who gave him God's words in Arabic. Those teachings were eventually compiled into the Koran. He began spreading his revelations, attracting both followers and enemies among the people of Mecca. Hostility from some Meccans drove him and his followers to Medina in 622, a migration that marks the beginning of the Muslim calendar. He returned to Mecca in 630. Although he was buried in Medina when he died two years later, Mecca is Islam's holiest city, and the Kaaba (KAH-AH-bah), a building covered with black cloth standing in the courtyard of the Great Mosque in Mecca, their holiest place.

Unlike Christianity, in which almost all sects have a universal leader (the pope, for example, in Roman Catholicism), Islam has no hierarchy. Each mosque has a leader or imam (EE-mahm) who is a spiritual guide and lecturer by virtue of his study of Islam and his perceived piety. The Koran and the teachings of Muhammad—called the Sunna (SOON-nah)—guide all aspects of Islamic life, including government, commerce, and life's daily details.

FIVE PILLARS OF ISLAM

These are the main religious principles:

Shahada (shah-HAH-dah)—the declaration that there is only one God and that Muhammad was his messenger.

Salat (sah-LAHT)—prayer five times daily, at sunrise, midday, afternoon, sunset, and later in the evening. Prayers are prescribed in both form and content. For example, the supplicant must face and bow toward Mecca, and women must cover their hair and entire bodies (except for the face, in some sects). Chanted calls to prayer are broadcast from all mosques and are part of life's daily rhythm.

Zakat (zah-KAHT)—an annual tithing of 2.5 percent of earnings above basic necessities. This alms money is used to build mosques and help the poor.

THE AMMAN MESSAGE

Although Muslim extremists are much feared, that fear has perhaps never been as great as it has since the infamous September 11, 2001 attack against the United States. Moderate Muslims (who are the overwhelming majority) do not condone the actions of terrorists and are very worried about the perceptions of the West and the destructive results of those perceptions. In an effort to assuage the fears of the West, King Abdullah II released what he called the "Amman Message" in November of 2004. In it he uses quotes from the Koran, Islam's holy book: "Islam upholds human life. There is to be no fighting against non-fighters; no assault on civilians and their properties, on children in their mothers' laps, on students in the schools, on older men and women. To assault the life of a human being is equivalent to assaulting the right to life of all—and this is one of the gravest sins."

Sawm (soom)—fasting during Ramadan, the ninth month of the Islamic year. During the fast, most Muslims do not eat, drink, or smoke from before dawn until after sunset. According to the instructions of the Koran, the evening begins and ends when one cannot distinguish a white thread from a black one in natural light. Those who are traveling or who fall ill during Ramadan may fast at some other time. The purposes of the fast are to purify one's soul and body and focus attention on God.

Hajj (hahj)—the pilgrimage to Mecca. This is required at least once in a lifetime if the person can afford it. Some Muslims make the pilgrimage many times, and others pay for poorer friends and relatives to go. The hajj is performed during the 7th and 10th days of the 12th month of the Islamic year.

OTHER RELIGIONS AND ISLAMIC SECTS

Jordan's Christians are predominantly Eastern Orthodox, followed by small numbers of Greek and Roman Catholics and various Protestant sects. Near the border with Syria there are small groups of Druze—a branch that broke off from mainstream Islam in the 10th century. Most Muslims regard the Druze as heretics. The group keeps its rituals and beliefs secret because traditionally only small groups of elites have full revelation of their religious teachings.

PRAYER RITUAL

The form of prayer is strictly prescribed by Islam. Supplicants first stand upright facing Mecca. The next moves are to:

- Open the hands.
- Touch the earlobes with the thumbs.
- Lower the hands and fold them, right hand over the left.
- Bow from the hips with hands on the knees.
- Straighten the body.
- Sink gently to the knees.
- Touch the ground (or floor) with hands, nose, and forehead, remaining 10–15 seconds in this position.
- Raise the body while kneeling, sitting on the heels.
- Press the hands, nose, and forehead to the ground again.
- Stand.

This ritual is called *raka* (RAH-kah) and is repeated several times.

Until the 1990s, the only Shi'a Muslims, or Shiites, in Jordan were the few thousand Chechens who were descended from those settled there by the Ottomans, and a few hundred Iraqi refugees. But now the estimated numbers of Iraqi Shi'a Muslims in Jordan are as high as 500,000. As in most cases of refugees, though, there is no way to get an accurate count.

Shiite Islam began shortly after the Prophet Muhammad died, when a group of his followers insisted that someone from his family must become the new Islamic leader. They chose Ali, the son of Muhammad's sister. The Sunni Muslims, on the other hand, believed a caliph (religious and political leader) should be elected as leader by a council of elders. The Shiite Muslims are now a minority group in Islam and have some beliefs and customs that differ from those of the Sunni Muslims. Throughout their history, Shi'a Muslims have suffered persecution from Sunni Muslims, who see them as heretics.

LANGUAGE

ARABIC ORIGINATES FROM THE SAME Semitic roots as Hebrew, Aramaic, and other ancient tongues of the Middle East. Arabs have developed a rich oral tradition, and many who are illiterate are still quite articulate. In the past, relatively few could read classical Arabic without difficulty, so the use of oral language became the ultimate art form to Arabs.

There are only two significantly different dialects in Jordan: city and rural, which is closer to standard Arabic. Educated urban Jordanians speak nearly the same variety as educated people in Damascus, Beirut, and Jerusalem, while villagers and the Bedouins speak a more guttural variety that more closely approximates the written form. There are vast differences in spoken Arabic, however, so much so that educated Jordanians might have trouble understanding an Algerian, for example. Written classical Arabic, because of its holy status in the Koran, has changed little in 1,200 years and is written in exactly the same way in every Arabic-speaking country.

Above: **A Jordanian man reads a newspaper in downtown Amman.**

Opposite: **Throughout Jordan many signs are written in Arabic. The use of Arabic for commercial purposes is common not only among Arab nations, but in most Muslim countries.**

AN ANCIENT LANGUAGE

The roots of Arabic go back thousands of years to the Phoenicians. Many centuries ago Arabs trading their wares in both Africa and India spread Arabic to such an extent that some languages of both areas now share words and characteristics with Arabic—particularly in Somali and Swahili.

A few English words are derived from Arabic as well. Examples are admiral, alcohol, algebra, check, checkmate, ghoul, lute, magazine, mummy, racket, safari, Sahara, sheriff, shish kebab, tariff, and zero.

The numerals, or figures, used in Europe and North America were also originally Arabic numerals. Arabs now use numerals that came to them from India, although there is a movement favoring the use of the original Arabic numerals again.

DIFFERENT STYLES

Linguists often assert that a people's view of life and their perspective of reality is strongly influenced by their native language. If this is true, the dramatic differences between the styles of communication in Arabic and English could produce a cultural gap and conflicting views of life. Thus it may be difficult for native speakers of either language to adjust to the speaking and writing styles of the other. This can lead to misunderstanding.

Anglo-Saxon speakers of English can often be identified by their understatement, precision, use of logic, and economy in words. They say what needs to be said very clearly and only once. Arabic speakers, on the other hand, demonstrate emotional appeal, overstatement or exaggeration, and repetition.

EMOTIONAL SPEECH Some scholars of Arab culture have said that Arabs are swayed more by words than ideas, and more by ideas than facts. Anglo-Saxon English speakers tend to use precise language in arguments, whereas most Arabs would prefer to use more flowery and emotional speech.

This difference creates communication difficulties between the two cultures. Most educated native English speakers have little regard for excessive emotional appeals, thinking that they reflect poor taste or are a sign of low intellect. Conversely, Arabs feel that the fact-filled arguments of a Westerner, spoken with seeming detachment, are distant and lack a human touch. Sociolinguists in the United States have, incidentally, found similar differences between the rhetorical styles and perceptions of some white and black Americans.

REPETITION AND HYPERBOLE   Writing styles are also dramatically different in English and Arabic. Compared with most American writing, Arabic is verbose, sprinkled with colorful descriptions. Information is repeated over and over in slightly different ways. One scholar said that Arabs are forced by their culture to overstate and exaggerate in all communication or risk being misunderstood.

Overstatement is also used in the display of warmth and hospitality. If an Arabic speaker says *"marhaba"* (MAR-hah-bah) or *"ahlan"* (ah-LAWN)—both meaning "hello"—to another, the answer will most often be *"marhabtain"* (MAR-hahb-tain) or *"ahlain"* (ah-LAIN)—"two hellos"—or *"ahlan wa sahlan"* (ah-LAWN wah sah-LAWN), meaning "hello and welcome." In other words, the response outdoes the initial greeting.

WORDS IN LIEU OF ACTION   Another quality of Arabic that most native English speakers fail to understand is the use of verbal threats. When Jordanians make threats, it is unlikely that they will carry out the action, although people from a different culture may react adversely. On the other hand, when Jordanian enemies say nothing, there is reason to worry. Among the more conservative Jordanians, "honor" and vengeance killings may occur with no warning if a family feels dishonored or insulted by the immoral or supposed immoral nature of a particular female member of the family. Such killings are illegal, but they live on because traditional families favor honor over the lives of their own wives and daughters.

> *"Arab conversation is peppered with blessings, which are like little prayers for good fortune, intended to keep things going well."*
>
> —*Margaret K. Nydell*

A bookstore on a street in Amman.

OTHER DIFFERENCES

In Arabic there is no equivalent of the English articles "a" and "an." Instead, *al* (ALL)—similar to the English definite article "the"—is used with nearly all nouns, as in "Would you like the coffee?" There are also other significant grammatical and sound differences between English and Arabic.

VERBS AND TENSES While English verbs usually indicate specific time, like the present or future, Arabic verbs are often not definite about time. Arabic has only two verb forms, the main ones being the "perfect" and "imperfect" (roughly, an action completed at the time of speaking, and a continuing or incomplete action from the past) tenses. There are verses in the Koran, for example, in which Allah acted in both the past and future at the same time. This apparent disregard for time and chronology is reflected in day-to-day living among the Arabs. Being late for an appointment is the norm, and few people get angry when they are kept waiting. Arabic does not have a present tense form of "to be." A person who is angry, for example, would say the Arabic equivalent of "I angry."

NOUNS AND ADJECTIVES All nouns in Arabic have either male or female forms, as they do in French and Spanish. Adjectives follow nouns and must agree in both number and gender.

LANGUAGE SEXISM In English the infinitive is "to" plus a base verb—to eat, to sleep. In Arabic, it is the pronoun "he" plus a past tense form—for example, "he ate" or "he slept." The present-tense verb form for the third person "he" (as in "he walks") is also different from all other verb forms. For example, in the dialect used by educated city people, *behki* (BEH-ki) means, "I speak," *btehki* (BTEH-ki) means "you speak" or "she speaks," while *ehki* (EH-ki) means "he speaks." The last is the form used in an Arabic dictionary. Words with associated meanings in Arabic use the same root consonants—there are words for "little boy," "children," and "giving birth" that all come from the same root. The word for "little girl," is the same word commonly used for "son" but is different from that used for "male child," while both "daughter" and "female child" are usually described by the same word.

THE SCRIPT

Arabic writing goes from right to left, and books begin from what a Westerner would call the back. There are no capital letters, but many letters change form depending on their position in a word—for example, beginning, end, or between two other letters. There are several different styles of writing, some of which are difficult to read. The ancient style of written Arabic is elaborate and decorative and forms the basis of calligraphy.

The style in newspapers and magazines, called modern standard Arabic script, is less elaborate but still difficult for Arabic learners because the marks that indicate vowels with short sounds and twin consonants are not used. Arabic, like Japanese, has both short and long vowels (short and long refer to the time lapse of their enunciation) and single and double consonants (also referring to the time lapse of their enunciation). Without these marks, the meanings of words can often be inferred only by context. Imagine reading English with short vowels not printed: "hat," "hit," "hot," and "hut" would all be spelled "ht!"

TONGUE TWISTERS

Several Arabic letters represent sounds that English does not have. Those below show the English letter or letters usually used in transliteration (writing a language using the alphabet of a different one). While the small letters "h," "s," "d," "t," and "z" carry the same sounds as in English, writing them in capital letters produces different sounds in transliteration.

- *H* (ha): a heavy "h" sound.
- *kh* (kha): similar to the "ch" sound in the German "Bach." The back of the tongue against the rear roof of the mouth does not block the air flow completely.
- *S* (sahd): a loose-tongued "s"; the tip of the tongue is not against the ridge behind the upper front teeth, but the front part of the tongue is flat against the front of the palate; somewhere between "sh" and "s" in English.
- *D* (dahd): a loose-tongued "d"; same instructions as for *S*.
- *T* (taa): a loose-tongued "t"; same as for *S* and *D*.
- *Z* (zaa): a loose-tongued "z"; same as above.
- *9* (ayn): a vowel formed with a narrowing of the throat. (Imagine saying "eye" with an "n" added to the end, and trying to "swallow" the "y" in the middle.)
- *gh* (ghayn): like a "g" without the back of the tongue actually touching the roof of the mouth; sometimes sounds like "l" or "r."
- *q* (qaa): a stop like a "k," but made in the throat; Amman's dialect substitutes the hamza for this.
- *'* (hamza): a glottal (voice box) stop usually represented in English transliterations as an apostrophe. An example is someone speaking in the Cockney dialect pronouncing bottle as "bo'le."

BODY LANGUAGE

Arab speakers stand very close to each other and use lots of flamboyant gestures—another form of overstatement. They also speak loudly. Unlike what may be perceived in the West, these characteristics do not represent aggression.

Jordanians use several head movements to communicate, with or without speaking. A quick upward movement of the head with raised eyebrows, often accompanied by closed eyelids and a click of the tongue, means "no." A downward nod to one side means "yes."

Hand gestures in Jordan are similar to those around the Mediterranean basin. The palm turned upward with the fingertips together forming a tent over the palm, the hand and forearm pumping up and down, and the arm flexing at the elbow means "Wait a minute." The palms up and open with arms out to the side and raised as if to lift something means "I don't know," or "I don't understand what's going on here." Open hands drawn quickly above the shoulders, palms facing the other person, means "That's my point!" Finally, the hands rubbed together quickly as if washing means "I'm finished with the matter."

OTHER LANGUAGES

Nearly all educated Jordanians speak some English, and those who are college-educated often speak it quite well. Even some Bedouins speak a little English since many of them depend heavily on tourism for personal income and have had a long historical association with the British. Only few people speak languages other than Arabic and English.

Arabs gesticulate a lot and can often convey their intentions without actually speaking.

ARTS

JORDANIAN ART IS mostly tradition-bound in design, materials, and colors. It comes predominantly in the forms of handicrafts such as rugs, fabrics, basketry, wood, and jewelry. The arts in Jordan also include the world of ideas as expressed in language and music.

ANCIENT ART

Both the Romans and the Greeks left their artistic footprints in the land that is now Jordan. The Roman art there consists of many ruins, as a result of the Roman occupation. These include many buildings and temples dedicated to the pre-Christian Roman pantheon, such as the citadel at Jerash. The later Byzantines (Greeks) left a legacy of Eastern Christian arts such as the mosaics of Christ and the Virgin Mary preserved in churches, monasteries, and convents.

ISLAM'S INFLUENCE ON ART

Traditional art in the Middle East reflects the role of Islam in daily living. Buildings and utensils were often decorated with religious motifs. There is no ban on figurative art in Islam per se, but many rulers have banned its use in religious art, based on the doctrine that Allah alone can create life. Instead, in circumstances where figurative art is forbidden, there is a proliferation of beautiful calligraphy that combines the elaborate shapes of the Arabic alphabet with verses from the Koran, resulting in ornate designs. Arab design also includes vast, intricate numbers of floral and geometric mosaic patterns, as can be seen on windows, walls, and doors of many splendid mosques, for example.

Above: **A seventh-century mosaic in the Church of Apostles in Madaba.**

Opposite: **An ancient mosaic map of Madaba.**

Dancers from the Circassian minority group perform an old folk dance at Jerash.

There is often lively improvisation between solo performers and their orchestras, somewhat similar to American jazz performances, a skill that is much appreciated by today's audiences.

Although some predominantly Muslim countries ban all kinds of representational art, Jordan does not. In fact, Jordan encourages and supports a wide variety of art, both traditional and modern. Many of the visual arts, however, are still strongly influenced by geometric designs and botanical scenes.

MUSIC

Jordanians respond in the same way to both music and narrative language. This is easy to understand, since music and language share certain characteristics in Arab culture. They are repetitive and exaggerated, yet full of subtleties, and are rich in stories about honor, family, and love.

Traditional Arabic music, like most music of Asia, is different from Western music. The latter uses half and whole notes with an eight-tone scale, while the former uses quarter notes and a five-tone scale. The music has a defining sound and beat and is highly elaborate. It has an intricate rhythm and is fairly ritualized in form. A single musical composition may last for half an hour. The instruments are usually played to accompany vocal music; there is very little purely instrumental Arabic music.

Classical Arabic music uses the oud (an instrument belonging to the lute family), the *kemancha* (ke-MAHN-cha), a type of violin with a gourd body and only one string, and small lap-held drums. In addition, two types of flute are commonly used in Jordan. One is called the *zamr mujwiz* (ZAH-mr MUJ-wiz), and the other is the *nay* (NAY).

Modern Arabic music often uses an orchestra of mostly European instruments, sometimes accompanied by a full choir. Audience participation is encouraged in the form of clapping and cheering. Nowadays, Western music is very popular, especially among teenagers, and several Jordanian pop and rock musicians play their versions of it. Others incorporate elements of both modern Western and classical Arabic music with some interesting effects. Indian, Persian, and northeast African music show characteristics that are similar to Arabic music because early Arabian traders spread their culture during the eighth and ninth centuries. Spanish flamenco music, for instance, has its origins in Arabic music.

LITERATURE

Jordanian literature is Arabic literature. Poetry—usually oral—has always been the primary form of literary expression in Arab culture, although scholarly and religious works are usually classified as literature, too. By the mid-20th century, strong feelings against foreign domination and Zionism found their way into poetic and literary works.

Books with religious themes being sold at an outdoor stall.

According to Arabic scholars, the literature can be divided into three main periods: classical, from ancient times to the 16th century; renaissance, from the 18th century until around the time of World War I; and modern.

CLASSICAL Arabic literature was strictly oral for hundreds of years, incorporating the poems and proverbs of the Bedouins. Many of these were eventually put into writing in the seventh and eighth centuries A.D.

A Jordanian Muslim girl reads the Koran in a mosque in Amman.

After the advent of Islam, all Arabic literature was filled with imagery from the Koran.

The earliest form of written poetry was called *qasidah* (kah-SEE-duh), meaning "purpose poem." These poems had between 20 and 100 verses and were usually an account of a journey undertaken by the sponsor of the poem. There would be a love poem prologue, followed by a long narrative of the journey, then an epilogue that flattered the host and heaped scorn upon his enemies. For centuries, Arab poetry followed this formula until it became too pompous and verbose, and then the form eventually died out.

Another form of classical poetry, called *ghazal* (GAH-zl), was a love poem that followed the form of the *qasidah* but was only five to 12 verses long. A form of verse known as *qit'ah* (KIT-uh) was less serious and used for jokes and word play.

Prose, although not nearly as popular or prevalent as poetry, took the form of simple true stories told in an exceedingly complicated and wordy manner, full of word play, double entendres, and complex imagery. These were called *maqamah* (mah-KAH-mah). Classical Arabic included no epic fiction of any kind, except for the translations of the Persian epic *Kitab Alf Layla wa Layla*, known to the world as *The Arabian Nights*. It became an Arabian classic, as these tales were adapted to the Arabic language, as well as being translated into many languages.

AN ANCIENT BEDOUIN FOLK TALE

In the search for new grazing pastures, a Bedouin tribe sent out a raven, a partridge, and a dove to look for grass. The raven returned quickly saying there was no grass to be found. The partridge and the dove came back later, saying that there was grass "soft as a lady's hair" within two days' journey.

The Bedouins traveled to where the partridge and the dove had seen the grass, and found it. To punish the raven, they colored it black to represent deceit. To reward the dove, they applied henna (a traditional Arab yellow ochre dye) on its feet, just as they would for a young Arab bride. To reward the partridge, they decorated its eyes with black lines of kohl (a dark-colored dye used as eyeliner).

RENAISSANCE After the 16th century, there was an interlude in the arts for a while. Ironically, the revival of the Arabic literary tradition began well after Napoleon Bonaparte conquered Egypt in the late 18th century. By the mid 19th century, after the modernization efforts of Egypt's sovereign, the Ottoman pasha Muhammad Ali, writers from all over the Arab world flocked to Cairo for its freedom of expression and came into contact for the first time with European literature. Although the literature of this renaissance was built upon foundations of classical Arabic literature, it began to incorporate thematic elements of European literature, becoming introspective and nationalistic. The most common form of writing in this period was the historical novel.

MODERN In the late 19th century, when European Jews began moving into Palestine (of which Jordan was still a part), Palestinians started to see the problems that such an influx could eventually cause and wrote about it. This literary trickle became a torrent after the creation of the state of Israel in 1948, after which most Palestinians became virtually homeless—both for daily shelter and a land to call their own.

Great literature is often born of tumult and disaster, and the displacement of hundreds of thousands of Palestinians was the flash point of modern Arabic literature. Surprisingly, however, the literature of the Palestinians did not simply become political and polemic; writers strove to show the moral bankruptcy and stagnancy of Arab culture in general. Many gifted women writers wrote about the real situation of women in the Arab world. Other writers felt it important to record the daily life of the people and a culture that had been nearly lost because of the Jewish control of Palestine.

The latter attempt became stronger after the 1967 war when the West Bank and Gaza Strip were occupied by the Israeli military. From then until Israel and the Palestine Liberation Organization signed their first agreement on the road to Palestinian self-rule, Palestinians who remained in the two conquered territories had no citizenship at all, no passports, and no constitutional rights. They were allowed to do only what the Israeli military authorities allowed them to. They were a people suffering in limbo.

Palestinian poetry of the late 20th century was described by one scholar as portraying, with subtlety and aesthetic sophistication, a genuinely existential situation, told in infinitely rich language. Despite the predominant use and importance of poetry, Palestinian literature also uses the short story and novel with great effect. Modern adaptations of Western literary models are gaining acceptance as well.

WRITERS

Some of the best known and most respected Jordanian-Palestinian writers are Fadwa Tuqan, Samira Azzam, Sahar Khalifeh, and Mona Sa'udi (all women); poets Ibrahim Abu Naab, Ibrahim Nasrallah, and Mustafa Wahbah at-Tal; and fiction writer Mahmoud Sayf ad-Din al-Irani. Al-Irani, who died in 1974, lived in Amman from 1942 and worked as a teacher and school inspector. He was a pioneer of the short story in Arabic literature, and his writing illustrates the inseparability of Jordanian and Palestinian cultures.

THE WORDS OF THE POETS

Here are words of some Jordanian-Palestinian writers that capture pictures of their situation.

Mona Sa'udi: "I find myself rootless and abandoned like a stone. Without love, there is no meaning to life nor to art. Why can't a man love a woman without having to choke her, to shut her up, controlling her mind, her dreams. . . . [H]ow can we love in freedom, not in oppression, only the woman is capable of that!"

Fadwa Tuqan (in response to her father's demand that she write more "political" poetry): "How and with what right or logic does father ask me to compose political poetry, when I am shut up inside these walls? I don't sit with men, I don't listen to their heated discussions, nor do I participate in the turmoil of life outside. I'm still not even acquainted with the face of my own country as I was not allowed to travel."

Fadwa Tuqan (in "Enough for Me"): Enough for me to die on her earth / be buried in her / to melt and vanish in her soil / then sprout forth as a flower / played with by a child from my country. / Enough for me to remain / in my country's embrace / to be in her close as a handful of dust / a sprig of grass / a flower.

Poem by **Ghassan Zaqtan**, "A Mirror": Two faces loom in the catastrophe / my father and his horses; a little moon / that we will capture sails above our house. / If only we could regain our childhood, / we'd imprison that moon / a while between our hands, / and when our hearts / opened, let it fly away.

Samira Azzam, from the short story "Bread of Sacrifice": "That spring, Ramiz learned about two things— love and war—and the first gave meaning to the second. War was not simply an enemy to kill voraciously. Rather, it was the assertion of the life of the land he loved and the woman he loved. Palestine was not only a sea with fishing boats, and oranges shining like gold, and not just olives and olive oil filling the big oil jars. It was Su'ad's black eyes as well. In Su'ad's eyes he saw all of Palestine's goodness."

Large, heavy gold necklaces, bracelets, anklets, earrings, and rings in elaborate designs are one way in which wealth can be invested and displayed at the same time.

Another famous Jordanian writer is Fadia Faqir, a Bedouin who writes novels about her homeland, in spite of living abroad. She delves into issues concerning gender politics, primarily supporting feminism in the Middle East. Her books are written in both English and Arabic.

Over the past two decades, a number of Arab writers has been experimenting with writing in "dialect," especially for dialogue. Conservative Muslims, however, feel that it is almost heretical to do so, for they believe the Arabic of the Koran to be sacrosanct—sacred and untouchable. As such, the sentiment is that it is all right to speak differently, but written language must conform to standard Arabic.

An interesting note is that the Arab League together with the United Nations Educational, Scientific, and Cultural Organization (UNESCO) cited Amman as the culture capital of the Arab world in 2002. This recognition acknowledges that Amman, and Jordan as a whole, emanates marvelous artistic energy.

HANDICRAFTS

Jordanian handicrafts reflect two main influences: the Bedouin and the Palestinian.

GOLD AND SILVER Bedouins have been creating elaborate jewelry for centuries, and their long tradition is reflected in modern adornments. Middle- and upper-class Jordanian women wear a lot of striking gold and gold-colored jewelry, including large hoop earrings and many

bracelets, some with extremely fine filigree designs. When these women wear scarves and veils, they often decorate them with chains and other jewelry. Necklaces with charms are very popular. In the past, most jewelry was sold at Jordanian souks and in shops that were owned and run by the artisans themselves. Today, this is still true in some of the older areas of cities.

WOODWORK Another typical Jordanian handicraft is wooden mosaic work. There are two basic types. One uses thin layers of factory-made veneers; in the more traditional style, each piece of wood, bone, or mother-of-pearl is cut and set by hand. Creating the latter is slow, painstaking work, but results in beautiful objects. The most common products are various sizes and shapes of boxes, trays, tables, and game boards. Jordanian artisans also carve objects from olive wood.

FABRICS Handweaving carpets and clothing (especially gowns and robes) are the main fabric arts in Jordan. These days, most carpets are made for sale to tourists. Weaving is done by women using simple handlooms and wool dyed in bright colors.

"As happens in backward societies where a woman's life revolves around trivialities, . . . the family environment offered me nothing; rather, it only increased my burden."

—Fadwa Tuqan, poet

107

Desert sand to take home. Colorful sand patterns carefully created and packed into glass bottles are popular with tourists.

Bedouin women and rural Palestinians still make traditional jackets, skirts, and various types of gowns for men and women. These are decorated with much embroidery, usually in cross-stitch. Palestinian embroidery is highly valued for its intricate, colorful designs that take months or years to create. The embroidery is also used on pillows.

BOTTLED SAND The skillful art of packing multicolored sand into small glass jars, forming designs that range from geometrics to plants and animals and scenes of the desert, is popular in Jordan. The design takes shape from the bottom of the container upward. Minute funnels are used to meticulously deposit small amounts of the sand into desired spots, a few grains at a time. The sand is continuously tamped down firmly to keep the design from crumbling. Once the jar is full and the artist is satisfied, the sand is given a final tamping and the jar opening is sealed with plaster.

GLASS BLOWING This is a minor craft in Jordan, used mostly to make glasses for tea (Arabs do not drink tea from cups), small dishes, and water pipes called *argheeleh* (ahr-GHEE-lay) in Arabic and "hubble-bubble" by most foreign visitors.

MODERN ARTS

Amman has numerous art galleries, and there is a significant number of painters and sculptors working in Jordan. Jordanian art reflects strong influences from contemporary American and European art but also embodies elements of Arab culture. Some Jordanian artists are very

USE OF RUGS

Nomads travel light for practical reasons. The ideal way to make a tent comfortable without a lot of heavy furniture is to use fabric. The typical Bedouin tent (and, often, village house) has large carpets that cover the entire enclosed ground, and these are piled with heaps of soft cushions on which the family sits and sleeps. The fabrics are woven from sheep, goat, and camel wool on horizontal, hand-built looms.

Small rugs are used over the carpets as prayer rugs. Each prayer rug has the geometric shape of an arrowhead at one end, and this is placed pointing toward Mecca when praying. These little carpets make a comfortable praying site, no matter where the believer might be when the call to prayer is heard. (*Pictured here, weaving of traditional Bedouin carpets.*)

Bedouin children inside their tent that is draped with traditional Bedouin carpets and rugs and decorated with furniture with ornate and colorful designs.

expressive, and their themes include love, the struggle for a Palestinian homeland, environmental destruction, traditional life, landscapes, and overpopulation. Unfortunately, Arab culture does not generally appreciate the visual arts beyond their decorative value, and most artists in Jordan struggle for economic and social survival to an even greater degree than their counterparts in the United States or Europe.

ARCHITECTURE

Islamic architecture features high ceilings, small windows, and thick walls. These help to keep the interior of buildings cool, even in hot weather. Traditional buildings face inward, overlooking an internal courtyard that often has a fountain. Domes and arches add a distinctive touch. Decorative elements include colorful mosaics and beautiful calligraphy.

"HUBBLE BUBBLE" WATER PIPES

Each *argheeleh* ranges from about 10 inches (25 cm) to 3 feet (90 cm) in height, usually has a handblown glass body and brass fittings, and stands on the floor. Sweet tobacco that has been cured with honey or sugared water is placed on a small tray on top of the *argheeleh*. A red-hot piece of charcoal is placed on top of the tobacco. At the bottom of the *argheeleh* is a water trap through which the smoke is sucked through a long, woven hose.

Sucking the smoke causes a pleasant bubbling sound that gives rise to its nickname of "hubble-bubble." The smoke smells sweet and feels cool in the mouth. The few scientific studies about the health consequences of smoking the water pipe, however, point to dangers that are similar to those associated with cigarette smoking. In spite of this, many Arab men (and also the more "liberated" women) still smoke the *argheeleh* after evening meals, especially when eating out in restaurants.

LEISURE

AS WITH ALL ARABS, rich or poor, urban or rural, socializing is the main source of entertainment and consumes a large part of every person's spare time. Jordanians generally are not interested in hobbies such as reading, tinkering with mechanical things, building things, engaging in sports, or other such activities, as many Americans and Europeans are into.

Above: **Time for a family meal. Meat dishes are favorites.**

Opposite: **The level of salt in the Dead Sea is so high that many go there for the pleasure of floating without much effort.**

DINING

Meals with friends and family, at home or in a restaurant, are often major social events. Lunch is the preferred time for socializing, as it is often the biggest meal of the day. Two to three hours can be spent socializing, eating, and drinking tea. Long dinners are common among affluent city dwellers.

Fridays, the official "weekend" day off in Jordan, are favorite days to spend outdoors. After attending prayer sessions in the mosque, many Jordanian men spend the entire day eating, talking, strolling the streets, or traveling short distances to restaurants outside town—especially during hot weather.

Being seen in their best clothes is important, and socializing is the main occasion for dressing up. Even conservative Muslim women often wear fashionable scarves and dresses. Young people scout for potential marriage partners at social gatherings—even if their efforts remain only in their dreams.

Unlike citizens of neighboring Syria and Lebanon, Jordanians do not mill around the streets on warm evenings. Amman's streets are quiet by 10 P.M. or 11 P.M., when most people are at home or in restaurants.

It is common for Jordanians to gather outside the Amman Central Library on a fine day to catch up with one another on the latest news.

OTHER ACTIVITIES

Art galleries and concerts are found mainly in Amman. Wealthy Westernized Jordanians attend concerts in droves, and their musical exuberance is usually obvious, even at classical music concerts. Arab people respond so strongly to music that most simply cannot sit still while a catchy tune is playing.

The country's art galleries are popular with some Jordanians, as is live theater. Most affluent Jordanians own videocassette recorders. For them, watching videos at home as entertainment is second only to socializing. There are many video stores with good selections of American and European films (with Arabic subtitles), and the videos are cheaper than in the United States or Europe. Most of the Arabic films are made in Egypt.

Magazines and newspapers from the United States, Europe, and all Arab countries are available and uncensored in Jordan. Such press freedom is highly unusual in an Arab country, and keeps literate Jordanians more in touch with the outside world than most other Arabs. Glossy picture magazines are also widely read.

Trips to the beach or outings to public parks are very much family affairs. Women often gather with other women for limited social activities or just to chat.

Guests received at home are greeted with a display of great hospitality. Foreign visitors are made to feel very welcome. Jordanians are happy to act as hosts and guides, and are eager to inform others about their culture and traditions.

FAVORITE PASTIMES

Many activities are gender-segregated in Jordan, although there is more social mixing among middle- and upper-class young people than in the past. Whole families may socialize together, or the men may join other men while the women and children mix with each other.

The more conservative Jordanians feel that a few public activities are taboo for women. These include standing on the street talking to friends, eating in restaurants without the presence of a male family member, going to a tea- or coffeehouse, and smoking in public. Men, on the other hand, spend most of their free time doing these very things with other men. Among more modern Jordanians, however, these taboos are not strictly observed, as many women today hang out on street corners and in restaurants, socializing their day away in the company of other female companions.

Older men, in particular, make a fine art of whiling away their time. They like to sit in teahouses drinking tea or Arabic coffee (a concentrated sweetened mixture served in small cups). Other pastimes are smoking the *argheeleh,* talking, or playing board games such as *mancala* and backgammon. Even shopkeepers spend a great deal of time indulging in various pastimes when customers are scarce. On Thursday nights, before the Friday day off, young men often hang out with male friends, talking, going to the movies—usually American action movies—or just watching young women passing by, who are almost always with their families.

While men hang out in the streets, tea shops, and cinemas, most women are usually working hard at home, shopping for the family's needs, or chatting with daughters, sisters, mothers, and neighbors. (*Pictured here, two Jordanian men playing backgammon in Madaba.*)

VERBAL GAME PLAYING

You might be wondering how people can have so much to talk about. In the Arabic language, what you say is often less important than how well you say it, and Arab men in particular can trade wits with each other for hours, using double entendres, one-liners, and scathing insults—all in jest. Particularly vivid and dramatically delivered insults are a source of delight, and their crafters are highly regarded for their masterful use of language and their speed at repartee. No offense is taken at such remarks. Favorite targets for insults are parents (especially mothers) and—believe it or not—the other person's religion.

Only the wealthy indulge in the sport of falconry. For them, fine falcons are prized possessions.

SPORTS

In an Arab country such as Jordan, the idea of competitive sport is relatively new, although camel and horse races have been held by Bedouins for centuries. The sport has gone professional, with races held on tracks outside the main cities in the late afternoon. Islam forbids gambling, but that does not reduce the excitement of a race.

As a spectator sport, soccer is the favorite among modern Jordanians. The country's official team, Al-Wihdat, which is often viewed as the rival to Saudi Arabia's Al-Faisaly team, was established in 1949 but did not qualify for the Fédération Internationale de Football Association (FIFA) World Cup until 1986. Regrettably, they have yet to reach a finals tournament. Despite their poor showing in FIFA matches, when a World Cup match is on, the men will be glued to their television sets no matter who is playing. Generally, only wealthy young Jordanians play any kind of organized sports once out of high school. The major cities have a few tennis courts, swimming pools, and running tracks, but no golf courses. There are several diving centers along the coast of Aqaba that are mainly popular among tourists.

Traditional wealthy men practice the ancient Arab sport of falconry, which involves hunting with falcons, a type of hawk. A few men still hunt in the desert, but since so much of Jordan's wildlife is endangered and thus off limits, hunting is not a serious sport.

MOVIES, RADIO, AND TELEVISION

Movie theaters show English-language movies as well as Middle Eastern staples. In Amman and elsewhere, cultural centers such as the Royal Theater, Balad Theater, and King Hussein Cultural Center hold frequent screenings of Jordanian movies. Since 1989 an annual European film festival has been held in Amman around May. Foreign cultural centers have regular film screenings there as well, contributing to an interesting balance between local and foreign cinematic influences.

There is a great variety of both radio and television programs in the country. Radio stations play current and classical Arabic music, some English-language programs, classical European music, and Western hits. The British Broadcasting Corporation's World Service can also be received. Radios are often played outdoors during warm weather, with the volume turned on high.

There are several Jordanian television stations, a few from Lebanon, and one or more—depending on geographic location—from Israel. Jordanian television broadcasts mainly in Arabic, but also in English. French programs are broadcast from Lebanon, and Hebrew programs from Israel. Jordanians are not limited to what they can receive locally from either their own or regional stations. They are avid watchers of international television via satellite, for they follow American soap operas, wrestling, news programs such as CNN, and soccer games from anywhere. Thus, they are in touch with the world as a whole.

Jordan's national soccer team takes on Iraq in a match in Amman. At the back of the spectators' stand is a giant poster of King Abullah. Most matches are telecast live for Jordanians.

117

FESTIVALS

JORDANIAN SOCIETY OBSERVES few actual festivals, since joyful celebrations are included in everyday wedding, birth, and religious traditions, which are all occasions for socializing. Of these, weddings are the most extravagant.

WEDDINGS

These are celebrated in different ways depending on whether the family is Christian or Muslim. They reflect the overriding importance of the family in Arab culture and are often elaborate events planned and executed without worrying about the expense.

In traditional Muslim families, males celebrate separately from females before the actual wedding ceremony. When a family does not have much money (particularly in rural areas), the men would celebrate in the streets and the women at home. The men clap, chant, and dance to the beat of a drum, while the women talk, laugh, and belly dance for each other. After the ceremony, there will be feasting, talking, and dancing—again, usually segregated by gender—that may last for several days.

Less traditional Muslims as well as Christians with lots of money may rent a hotel ballroom and eat, drink, and dance all night, usually with the men and women celebrating together.

Above: **Modern couples often choose to marry in Western-style clothes.**

Opposite: **The ancient amphitheater of Jerash. Every year the famous and much-anticipated Jerash Festival is held for the display of local and international art performances.**

119

HEAD AND SHOULDERS ABOVE THE CROWD

Before a wedding ceremony, conservative Muslim men perform a unique ritual in the streets. Wearing white skullcaps, they stand in a circle around a mosque leader who is standing on the shoulders of one or two other men. The leader leans down toward the crowd of onlookers and waves his arms in time to a rhythm tapped out on a drum and the clapping of hands. He also chants verses from the Koran and bestows blessings upon the new couple. It is particularly important to ask for many sons to be born of the marriage. The chanting can last up to half an hour as the group parades down the street. After this ritual, the bridegroom is escorted to the door of his bride's home (or wherever the women's party is going on) and nudged in backward through the door.

A Jordanian man selling special sweets offered during Prophet Muhammad's birthday.

RELIGIOUS FESTIVALS

For both Muslims and Christians, religious events are the second-biggest celebrations after wedding parties, with Muslim festivals being both the longest lasting and the liveliest.

MUSLIM FESTIVALS Although not a festival per se, Ramadan—the ninth month of the Islamic calendar, during which devout Muslims fast from sunrise to sunset—includes feasting in the daily evening meal called *iftar* (IF-tar). It also includes special mosque services and the *tarawih* (TA-ra-weeh) prayer ritual, which is performed every evening as part of a great deal of socializing and public activity after dark. For *iftar*, special dishes are prepared that are eaten only during Ramadan. Large quantities of food are served, and the extended family is present. During the last few days of Ramadan, clothing stores stay open especially late so that people can buy the new clothes they will wear during the three-day holiday called Eid (ID), that follows the end of Ramadan. To an observer, Ramadan evenings have all the attributes of mini festivals.

Eid is observed twice. The first time occurs immediately after Ramadan; the second, after a hajj, or pilgrimage. For these festivals, people eat special foods (especially sweets) and stay up all night socializing with extended family members and friends. Carnival rides are set up in city and village parks, horses and donkeys are rented for children to ride in the streets, and everyone wears new clothes. The first Eid seems more like a festival than the second. Perhaps this is because most Muslims fast during Ramadan, but only a small number make the hajj in any one year. During both Eid festivals, few businesses or shops are open, government offices and schools are closed, and the rich go on vacation to resort areas.

The dates for Eid are determined by the Muslim lunar calendar, which is based on the first sighting of the moon. Even though they are officially celebrated over three days, it is common for some businesses, schools, and embassies to close for a whole week.

Portrait of a three-handed Virgin Mary in a church in Madaba.

CHRISTIAN CELEBRATIONS   Christmas is celebrated by all Christians, just as Easter is celebrated according to the Eastern Orthodox calendar by all of Jordan's Christian denominations. Because of the small number of Christians, the celebrations are low key and there is little festivity in the streets. Government offices, schools, and Christian businesses are closed for these observations.

One will not find Christmas caroling, decorated streets, Christmas trees, or Easter egg hunts in public, but some businesses are starting to decorate their stores, hoping to cash in on the festive moods. The stores are also generally busier, catering to shoppers who want to find gifts for loved ones and friends.

Christmas and Easter holidays are celebrated in the homes of believers in much the same way as they are in the West, with special meals, gift giving, new clothing, Christmas trees, and decorations. The churches hold special masses or other services, and there is much rejoicing.

OTHER CELEBRATIONS Jordanians celebrate, with special music and dancing, other events such as births, circumcisions, plowing, planting, and harvesting. These are governed by tradition, and the entire family takes part in the rituals.

Tourists and churchgoers in the Church of Saint George in Madaba.

TOURIST ATTRACTIONS

In order to generate some much-needed tourist income for the country, Jordan sponsors and publicizes several events. One is the camel and horse festival, which includes races with these animals, and special talent and breed shows. Another is a colorful hot-air balloon festival in Wadi Rum. Concerts are held occasionally in Amman's Roman theater.

There are two major festivals every year. The Jerash Festival for Culture and Arts takes place every August over a two-week period and includes daily presentations by Jordanian, Arab, and international folk music troupes and performers, poetry readings, ballet, Shakespearean theater, and art shows. The Aqaba Sports Festival held in mid-November includes world-class competition in water-skiing and other aquatic sports.

DANCING FOR LIFE

Few of the traditional dances performed in Jordan are organized presentations for which people buy tickets and sit to watch. They are usually performed at family celebrations by ordinary people in the same costumes and with the same movements that have been in existence for many generations. The most common forms of rhythmic accompaniment for dancing are pounding feet, clapping hands, and the playing of small drums. One dance, the *debkah* (deb-KAH), is Jordan's most popular. It resembles the Spanish flamenco, which, itself, started with dances taken to Spain by Arab conquerors 1,200 years ago.

Bedouins have their own dance, called the *sahjeh* (SAH-jeh), illustrating grand stories of heroic deeds. Circassians have a unique sword dance, accompanied by music, and there is a special dance troupe that performs for the public. The troupe has appeared on television and traveled abroad to perform, and its music is sometimes broadcast on Jordanian radio stations.

A Jordanian woman in traditional dress that is worn during important festivals and by dancers performing traditional festive dances.

123

FOOD

JORDANIAN FOOD IS SIMILAR to that of its neighbors Syria, Lebanon, and Iraq. Lamb is consumed in large quantities, and yogurt, chicken, bulgur (cracked wheat), parsley, eggplant, tomatoes, rice, and flat bread make up most of the average person's diet. The usual seasonings are garlic and mint. Dates are also important when in season and are used in some traditional sweets. The Ottoman Turks introduced some of the basic recipes during their long occupation of the area.

MEALS

Breakfast is usually eaten quite early, especially in Muslim families, because they get up at dawn to pray, and then eat afterward. Schoolchildren also start the day early, around 6 A.M. in the summer. This means that the mother and older sisters must get up early to prepare food. The largest meal of the day generally is lunch, which is served around 2 P.M. Dinner is light (except during Ramadan, special feasts, or when eating out) and is always eaten after 8 P.M. Coffee or tea follows every meal, regardless of whether the meal is eaten at home or in a restaurant.

TYPES OF FOOD

Jordanian food is hearty fare with lots of meat—mostly lamb and chicken—and thick savory dips that are scooped up and eaten with flat bread. Perhaps the most ubiquitous food item in Jordan is the olive, which is eaten with every meal as well as for snacks. Olives are available in dozens of varieties, ranging from enormous to tiny, from yellow to black, from bitter and dry to sweet and juicy, and from crunchy to soft. Olive oil, clarified butterfat called ghee, and lard rendered from the tail of fat-tailed sheep are used extensively in or on nearly all food.

Opposite: **Jordanian shoppers and vendors in a fruit and vegetable market in Amman.**

MAIN COURSES Breakfast is always light, and usually consists of cheese, olives, and bread—sometimes with jam. For lunch, the national—and maybe the most common dish—is an old Bedouin concoction called *mansaf* or *mansif* (MAHN-seef). This is made from lamb, yogurt, and rice and simmered for a long time. The Bedouins still eat it the traditional way—scooped up with bread or the fingers—but some modern Jordanians use a spoon. *Kusa mahshi* (KOO-sa MEH-she), a regional favorite, is a small zucchini-type squash that is cored and then stuffed with a rice-meat mixture and served as a treat.

Various other dishes with lamb, vegetables, rice, and lemon are also common. Marinated and barbecued chicken, called *shishtou* (shish-TA-oo), is popular, especially among city people.

Certain foods are made in large quantities and preserved in jars to last for a year or more. One such example is the *maqdous* (MUK-too), made of small eggplants stuffed with spiced meat and then pickled.

THE TRIMMINGS Before the main course is served at home, hors d'oeuvres such as shish kebabs, small, spicy meatballs, cheese, pickles, and olives might typically be served. Along with the main course people often have soup—usually either lamb broth, vegetable, or lentil—and a salad called *fatoush* (fah-TOOSH) that includes mint and bits of yesterday's flat bread fried crisp in oil. In Arabic restaurants, the hors d'oeuvres consist of various creamy dishes made from eggplant, chickpeas (garbanzo beans), and yogurt. The dips are eaten by scooping them up with bits of fresh flat bread. Salads are also popular, especially one made with yogurt, cucumber, mint, and garlic.

Favorite drinks are canned carbonated beverages, tea, coffee, and *laban* (LAY-bun)—a yogurt, water, and garlic drink. *Laban* is the Arabic word for yogurt. All meals, whether at home or in traditional Arab restaurants, are accompanied by trays of olives, raw vegetables such as peppers and carrots, pickles, and sometimes cheese made from goat's or sheep's milk.

SWEETS AND SNACKS

Although Western-style treats such as ice cream and pudding have become popular among Jordanians, the locals have, in fact, their own sweet treats, such as Jordanian ice cream, which is gummy and topped with pistachios, and the dense, traditional Arab confections such as baklava, that remain all-time favorites. Baklava is delicious but rich and very sweet. These sweets include a lot of chopped nuts (especially pistachios), coconut, and sugar syrups. Equally popular for desserts are trays of fresh fruit such as melons, bananas, grapes, apricots, peaches, and plums.

INTERNATIONAL FOODS

Jordanians, having been exposed to the West in various ways for several generations, have developed a taste for nontraditional foods. Aqaba has a Chinese restaurant as well as Italian and several seafood establishments that serve European-style menus. Amman has numerous Italian, Chinese, Japanese, French, and Spanish restaurants dotted all over the city. The luxury hotels throughout Jordan serve a large variety of cuisines, and breakfast buffets that include Arab, American, and European foods are tasty fares for the locals as well as tourists.

ARABIAN FAST FOOD

There are now many international fast-food chains in Jordan, and there is a delicious local version of fast food. Small shops and street vendors make something like a sandwich (but is more like a burrito or a "wrap"), which they call *shawarma*. It consists of thinly sliced lamb or chicken rolled up with garnishes and sauce in a small piece of flat bread. Other shops sell falafel (fah-LAW-fel) sandwiches—crumbled falafel (a deep-fried croquette of ground chickpeas or fava beans and spices) mixed with yogurt, parsley, and other foodstuffs, and also rolled up in flat bread. Chicken shops sell whole roasted birds stuffed with rice or cracked-wheat mixtures, as well as fried chicken and french fries.

Also, depending on the season, vendors with colorfully decorated carts on street corners sell unripened almonds (a sour treat dipped in salt before eating), boiled corn on the cob, roasted chestnuts, fresh pistachios, unripened plums, and various other treats.

IN A JORDANIAN KITCHEN

Middle- and upper-class Jordanians equip their kitchens in a style similar to European or American kitchens. They often have appliances such as dishwashers, food processors, and microwave ovens. Poorer people, and those who are more traditional, use only basic utensils that require much muscle power and human energy.

Jordanians buy large amounts of food items such as eggplant, coring them to make stuffed eggplant dishes. They do similar operations with other vegetables. Women always do this work, and a mother who has one or two daughters to help with the chores is indeed fortunate. In traditional homes, men do not help to prepare food.

PROLIFIC PALMS

The most common type of palm tree in Jordan is the date palm. It grows primarily in the desert, wherever there are oases or where seasonal water collects. Each tree can produce up to 600 pounds (270 kg) of fruit a year. The dates are vivid red-orange until they ripen, after which they turn a very dark brown.

The date palm grows rows of new leaf stalks every year. The old stalks are harvested and woven into baskets and sturdy mats. The leaves, too, can be woven into lighter-weight mats (for tabletops, for example), small baskets, and even sandals. Traditional Bedouins derived a large part of their diet from date palms, and used the stalks and leaves to make many useful household products. Today, most woven products from the trees are sold to tourists. (*Pictured here, a man sells dates in a vegetable market in Amman.*)

DAILY SHOPPING

Arabs, men and women, do their shopping daily to procure their food and other domestic needs. Jordan now has numerous large supermarket chains such as Safeway and the international Carrefour supermarkets. They provide Amman residents, as well as those living in the other major cities, the opportunity to buy turkeys from the United States, asparagus from France, and various other goods that are not available in Arab souks—marketplaces where local products are obtained. Most other stores in Jordan are small by Western standards and usually sell a narrow range of foods—grocery stores sell canned goods and packaged goods; fruit and vegetable vendors sell local and some imported produce; while butchers often have only chicken or lamb.

There are four types of bakeries: one for the traditional Arab flat bread, one for French-type baguettes, one for elaborately decorated European-style sweets, and another for traditional Arab confections. Since most groceries are bought fresh every day, shopping takes a great deal of time. In some conservative Muslim families, the fathers and sons do all the shopping to avoid having their women dealing with other men.

MANSAF

Mansaf or *mansif* is a traditional Bedouin food for special feasts and is unique to Jordan. The recipe does not have to be strictly followed, and each family and tribe makes it to their own taste, but the dish is basically a slab of Arab flat bread with a pyramid of rice on top of it; lamb is arranged over the rice and is covered with pine nuts, almonds, and a yogurt sauce. Arabs eat this with their right hands, not with knives and forks.

1 cup (230 g) whey (dried yogurt); if whey cannot be found, plain yogurt can be used
2 cups (455 g) long-grain rice
2 ½ cups water for rice
2 pounds (1 kg) of lamb, boneless, cubed
2 medium onions, diced
2–3 slices of Arabic flat bread (pita bread may also be used)
A handful or two each of pine nuts and toasted almonds

First, soak whey in water for one hour, then mash it and let it stand for a while to dry it out. Alternatively, if yogurt is used, spread it out and dry it for a bit. Start cooking the rice. Next, put the lamb and the onion into a large pot, just cover with water, and bring to a boil. Reduce heat and simmer until meat is fairly well done. Remove meat and add the dried whey or yogurt to the broth and simmer until it thickens a bit (cornstarch or flour may be added to thicken, if desired). Add the meat again and simmer the mixture until the meat is well done.

When the rice is cooked, cover a large tray with two or three slices of Arabic flat bread, then mound the rice pyramid-style on top of the bread. Arrange the pieces of meat on the rice, then sprinkle with the pine nuts and almonds. Pour enough of the hot whey broth over it to make it slightly moist. This recipe serves four.

MAP OF JORDAN

ECONOMIC JORDAN

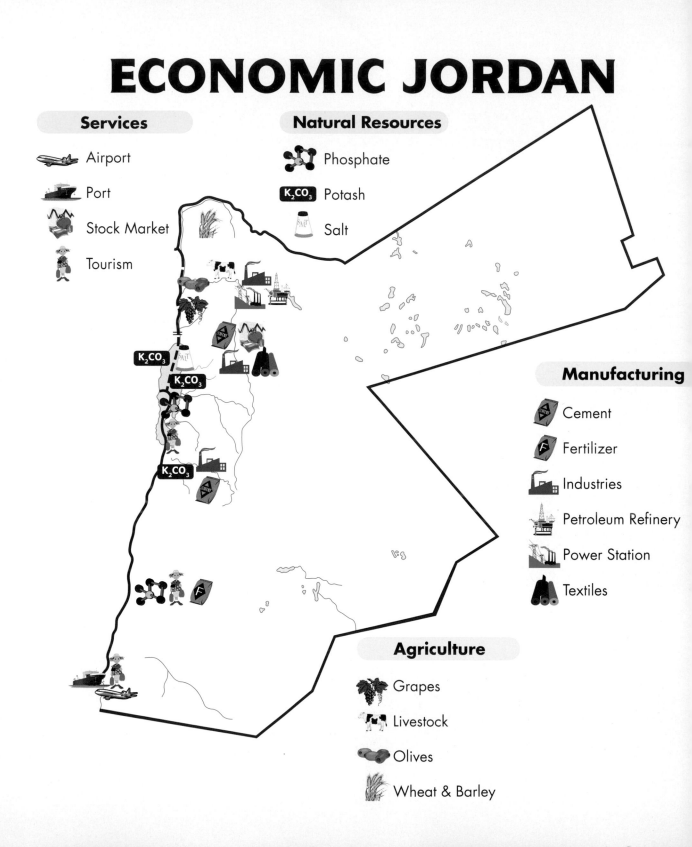

Services
- ✈ Airport
- 🚢 Port
- 📈 Stock Market
- 👜 Tourism

Natural Resources
- Phosphate
- K₂CO₃ Potash
- Salt

Manufacturing
- Cement
- F Fertilizer
- Industries
- Petroleum Refinery
- Power Station
- Textiles

Agriculture
- Grapes
- Livestock
- Olives
- Wheat & Barley

ABOUT THE ECONOMY

GROSS DOMESTIC PRODUCT (GDP)
$28.9 billion (2006 estimate)

GDP GROWTH RATE
6 percent (2006 estimate)

GDP PER CAPITA
$4,900 (2006 estimate)

GDP BY SECTOR
Agriculture 3.6 percent, industry 30.5 percent, services 65.9 percent (2006 estimates)

INFLATION RATE
6.3 percent (2006 estimate)

POPULATION
6,053,200 (2007 estimate)

POPULATION GROWTH RATE
2.412 percent (2007)

WORKFORCE
1.52 million (2006 estimate)

WORKFORCE BY OCCUPATION
Agriculture 5 percent, industry 12 percent, services 83 percent (2001 estimates)

CURRENCY
Jordanian dinar (JOD)
USD 1 = JOD 0.708 (2006)

UNEMPLOYMENT RATE
Official statistic: 15.4 percent
Unofficial statistic: 30 percent (2006)

POPULATION BELOW POVERTY LINE
30 percent (2001 estimate)

MAIN AGRICULTURAL PRODUCTS
Wheat, barley, citrus, tomatoes, melons, olives, sheep, goats, poultry

MAIN INDUSTRIES
Textiles, phosphate mining, fertilizers, pharmaceuticals, petroleum refining, cement, potash, inorganic chemicals, light manufacturing, tourism

EXPORTS
Clothing, phosphates, fertilizers, potash, vegetables, manufactured items, chemicals

IMPORTS
Crude oil, textile fabrics, machinery, transportation equipment, manufactured goods

TELECOMMUNICATIONS
Main telephone lines: 628,200 (2005 estimate)
Mobile telephone lines: 3.02 million (2005 estimate)
Internet hosts: 3,441 (2006 estimate)
Internet users: 629,500 (2005 estimate)

AIRPORTS
17; 15 with paved runways, 2 without

ROADWAYS
4,660 miles (7,500 km) (2004 estimate)

CULTURAL JORDAN

ROMAN RUINS OF JERASH
This is the site of well-preserved Roman ruins—the famous ruins of Jerash, among the best preserved in the world.

UMM AL-JIMAL
Town of Umm al-Jimal (OOM al jiMAL), where well-preserved ruins of the Byzantine/early Islamic town can be found.

BLACK DESERT
A part of the va
Syrian Desert, th
is an expanse
desert and steppe

AZRAQ OASIS
Azraq Oasis is the only permanent body of wa
in 46,000 square miles (119,140 sq km) of dese
Home to huge numbers of animal species and a stop-
point for multitudes of migrating birds.

OMAYYAD CASTLES
Site of six Omayyad castles of the seventh and eig
centuries; good examples of early Islamic architect
and art.

JORDAN RIVER VALLEY
Among the first-known sites of civilization and site
first cultivated wheat.

AMMAN, CAPITAL CITY
Site of well-preserved Roman ruins (the amphithea
is still used for various events) and remains of anci
Ammonite capital Rabbath Ammon. It also hosts ma
museums, art galleries, movie theaters, and oth
metropolitan cultural points of interest.

DEAD SEA
The lowest point on earth and one of the saltiest se
on earth; one cannot sink in the water because of
high salt content.

RUINS OF PETRA
Magnificent, unique ruins of Petra; mixture
Nabatean, Greek, and Roman structures cut into a
built onto sheer cliffs of rose-colored sandstone in
very narrow gorge.

WADI RUM
Famous in the West as a backdrop for the movie
Lawrence of Arabia; exotic landscape of flat desert
floor with hilly knobs protruding. Also site of annual
hot-air balloon race.

PORT OF AQABA
Jordan's only port on the Red Sea. Big tourist
area, especially for travelers from the Middle
East and divers who want to view the spectacular
underwater sights.

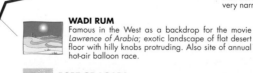

ABOUT THE CULTURE

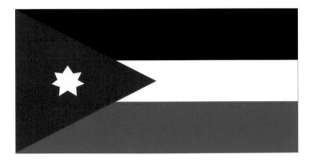

OFFICIAL NAME
Hashemite Kingdom of Jordan

FLAG
Black stripe on top, white in middle, green on bottom; starting in left top and bottom corners, a red triangle with its point about 40 percent across the flag in the white stripe; in the center of the red triangle features a small, seven-pointed white star. The seven points on the star represent the seven verses of the opening sura (al-Fatiha) of the Koran. They symbolize faith in one God, humanity, national spirit, humility, social justice, virtue, and aspirations.

NATIONAL ANTHEM
"Long Live the King!" (Arabic, "As Salam al Malaki al Urdoni")

CAPITAL
Amman

OTHER MAJOR CITIES
Zarqa, Irbid, Ma'an

DATE OF INDEPENDENCE
May 25, 1946

ETHNIC GROUPS
Arab (non-Bedouin), Bedouin, Circassians, Chechens, Armenians

OFFICIAL LANGUAGE
Arabic, but English is widely understood among upper and middle classes

LITERACY RATE
Total: 91.3 percent; females 86 percent, males 96 percent.

RELIGIOUS GROUPS
Sunni Muslims, Shi'a Muslims, Christians

LIFE EXPECTANCY
Total population: 78.6 years; females 81 years, males 76 years

FERTILITY RATE
2.6 children born to every Jordanian woman (2007 estimate)

INFANT MORTALITY RATE
16.2 deaths per 1,000 live births (2007 estimate)

BIRTHRATE
20.7 births per 1,000 Jordanians

DEATH RATE
2.7 deaths per 1,000 Jordanians

TIME LINE

IN JORDAN	IN THE WORLD
	1914 World War I begins.
	1939 World War II begins.
1946 Independence gained from Great Britain; new constitution gives Abdullah nearly total control of country; Abdullah crowns himself king.	**1945** The United States drops atomic bombs on Hiroshima and Nagasaki.
1948 State of Israel is established and thousands of Palestinians flee to West Bank and Jordan.	**1949** The North Atlantic Treaty Organization (NATO) is formed.
1950 Jordan annexes West Bank.	
1951 Abdullah is assassinated and his son Talal is crowned.	
1952 Talal is declared mentally unfit to rule and is replaced by his son Hussein.	**1957** The Russians launch Sputnik.
1963 King Hussein dissolves parliament.	**1966–69** The Chinese Cultural Revolution
1974 Hussein recognizes PLO as the Palestinian people's sole legitimate representative.	
1984 Parliament convenes for first time in 21 years.	
1986 New electoral law is passed, creating small constituencies—Christians, Palestinians, and Circassians/Chechens. Palestinians in refugee camps also given representation.	**1986** Nuclear disaster at Chernobyl in Ukraine
1988 Hussein formally cedes Jordan's claim on West Bank to Palestinians.	
1989 First parliamentary election is held in 22 years.	

IN JORDAN	IN THE WORLD
1991	**1991**
Gulf War breaks out. Jordan remains neutral and is flooded with refugees from Iraq and Palestinians from Kuwait.	Breakup of the Soviet Union
1993	
New elections law passed and 15 political parties take part in elections; first multiparty elections in 37 years. Jordan and Israel declare peaceful coexistence at ceremonies in White House in Washington, D.C.	
1997	**1997**
Laws restricting freedom of press passed; Islamic political parties boycott legislative elections on grounds they were unfair to Islamists.	Hong Kong is returned to China.
1999	
Hussein dies at 63, only a few days after bone marrow transplant for non-Hodgkin's lymphoma; son Abdullah II enthroned; promises to work on creating more open government and freedom of expression.	
2000	
Jordan joins World Trade Organization; signs free trade agreement with the United States—the first between the United States and an Arab country; signs association agreement with the European Union.	
2001	**2001**
Parliament's term expires without new elections; government fears sympathy for Palestinians' new conflict with Israel would give Islamist parties victory.	Terrorists crash planes in New York, Washington, D.C., and Pennsylvania.
2003	**2003**
Parliamentary elections give king's supporters a majority; Islamist parties get only 18 seats out of a total of 275.	War in Iraq begins.

GLOSSARY

al Hamdullah (ahl HAHM-dool-lah)
Phrase meaning "Thank Allah"

argheeleh (ahr-GHEE-lay)
"Hubble-bubble" water pipes for smoking

Badoo (BAH-doo)
"Desert dweller," the Arabic name for the Bedouins

corral
Enclosure for cattle or horses

Eid (ID)
Three-day religious celebration and holiday at the end of the fasting month of Ramadan; also the holiday following the Muslim pilgrimage to Mecca

fatoush (fah-TOOSH)
Salad with mint and flat bread fried crisp in oil

Hejaz (hee-JAZZ)
Provincial area of western Saudi Arabia, along the Red Sea and Gulf of Aqaba, formerly an independent kingdom; in 1932 it united with the sultanate of Nejd to form Saudi Arabia

insha'allah (in-SHAH'-ahl-LAH)
A phrase commonly quoted that means "God willing" when talking about the future.

Kaaba (KAH-AH-bah)
The holy building covered with black cloth standing in the courtyard of the Great Mosque in Mecca

kaffiyeh (kah-FEE-yay)
Traditional Arab headdress for men

laban (LAY-bun)
Yogurt, water, and garlic drink; also refers to plain yogurt.

Levant
The name for the lands on the eastern Mediterranean shore that is now occupied by Lebanon, Syria, and Israel

maha (MAH-hah)
Oryx (literally "crystal"), a type of antelope

mansaf or **mansif** (MAHN-seef)
Meal made of lamb and yogurt, simmered for a long time and eaten with rice and flat bread, scooped up with the fingers

maqdous (MUK-too)
Eggplant stuffed with spiced meat and then pickled

raka (RAH-kah)
Prayer ritual

Shari'a (shah-REE-ah)
Islamic law

sunna (SOON-nah)
Teachings and examples set by the Prophet Muhammad

wadi (WAH-dee)
Canyon

Zionism
Political movement for the establishment and support of a national homeland for the Jews in Palestine, now concerned chiefly with the development of the modern state of Israel

FURTHER INFORMATION

BOOKS

Auge, Christian and Jean-Marie Dentzer. *Petra: Rose Red City (New Horizons)*. London: Thames and Hudson Limited, 2000.

Insight Guides. *Jordan Insight Guide*. Duncan, SC: American Map-Langenscheidt Publishing Group, 2005.

Mayhew, Bradley. *Jordan (Lonely Planet Country Guide)*. Sixth edition. Oakland, CA: Lonely Planet Publications, 2006.

Teller, Matthew. *The Rough Guide to Jordan*. Third edition. New York: Penguin Group, Rough Guides, 2006.

WEB SITES

ABC News: Dead Sea Is Dying. http://abcnews.go.com/GMA/story?id=1332897

AllRefer Channels. http://reference.allrefer.com/encyclopedia/J/Jordan-history.html

Animal Info—Jordan. www.animalinfo.org/country/jordan.htm

Arab Countries: The Country and People of Jordan (includes many links to other related sites about the country). www.hejleh.com/countries/jordan.html

Complete Petra, The. www.isidore-of-seville.com/petra/index.html

Dead Sea Guide: Healing Effects of the Region. www.dead-sea.net/healing.htm

Environment News Service: Vanishing Jordan River Needs Global Rescue Effort. www.ens-newswire.com/ens/may2006/2006-05-16-10.asp

Focus Online Magazine: Focus on Jordan. www.focusmm.com/jordan/jo_anamn.htm

Foreign Ministry, The Hashemite Kingdom of Jordan: Jordan First. www.mfa.gov.jo/pages.php?menu_id=374

Haaretz.com: Jordan Grapples with End of Iraq War. www.haaretz.com/hasen/pages/ShArt.jhtml?itemNo=336093&contrassID=2&subContrassID=5&sbSubContrassID=0&listSrc=Y

Hashemite Kingdom of Jordan: Al Mamlakah al Urduniyah al Hashimiyah, former Transjordan. http://zhenghe.tripod.com/j/jordan/

Hashemite Kingdom of Jordan, The: The People of Jordan. www.kinghussein.gov.jo/people1.html#The%20Circassians

Hashemite Kingdom of Jordan travel guide: Food/drinks and nightclubs. www.jordan-travel-guide.de/jordanfood.html

iExplore: Jordan Travel Guide. www.iexplore.com/res/d.jhtml?destination=Jordan&type=Dining

Jordan Human Development Report 2004: Building Sustainable Livelihoods. www.undp-jordan.org/JordanHumanDevelopmentReport/tabid/81/Default.aspx

Jordan River Foundation: Historical trees of Jordan. www.jordanriver.jo/Publications.asp

Jordan Times, The (English language newspaper). www.jordantimes.com/thu/index.htm

Khalil Sakakini Cultural Center (visual arts, literature, etc.). www.sakakini.org/literature/literature.htm

Lexicorient.com, Encyclopedia of the Orient: Jordan: Health and Education. http://lexicorient.com/e.o/jordan_3.htm

LotusOrganics.com: Jordan: A River of Garment Worker Tears. www.lotusorganics.com/articles/Jordan GarmentWorkers.aspx

Nation by Nation: Population—Jordan. www.nationbynation.com/Jordan/Population.html

Nodeworks Encyclopedia. http://pedia.nodeworks.com/J/JO/JOR/Jordan

OneWorld.net. http://uk.oneworld.net/guides/jordan/development

Petra. www.raingod.com/angus/Gallery/Photos/MiddleEast/Jordan/Petra/

Umm el-Jimal. www.calvin.edu/academic/archaeology/uj/uj.htm.

What's Up in Jordan? http://ajloun.blogspot.com/

West Semitic Research Project: Dead Sea scrolls. www.usc.edu/dept/LAS/wsrp/educational_site/dead_sea_scrolls/copperscroll.shtml

Wild World—Ecoregion Profile: The Red Sea. www.worldwildlife.org/wildworld/profiles/g200/g231.html

World Atlas: Jordan—History, Geography, and Economic Information. www.world-atlas.net/Jordan

World Factbook, The (U.S. CIA). www.cia.gov/cia/publications/factbook/index.html

ZNet: Iraqi Refugees in Jordan. www.zmag.org/content/showarticle.cfm?SectionID=15&ItemID=8373

BIBLIOGRAPHY

ABC News: Dead Sea Is Dying. http://abcnews.go.com/GMA/story?id=1332897

AllRefer Channels. http://reference.allrefer.com/encyclopedia/J/Jordan-history.html

Animal Info—Jordan. www.animalinfo.org/country/jordan.htm

Arab Countries: The Country and People of Jordan (includes many links to other related sites about the country). www.hejleh.com/countries/jordan.html

BBC News—Jordan (Country Profile). http://news.bbc.co.uk/1/hi/world/middle_east/country_profiles/828763.stm

Complete Petra, The. www.isidore-of-seville.com/petra/index.html

Dead Sea Guide: Healing Effects of the Region. www.dead-sea.net/healing.htm

Environment News Service: Vanishing Jordan River Needs Global Rescue Effort. www.ens-newswire.com/ens/may2006/2006-05-16-10.asp

Focus Online Magazine: Focus on Jordan. www.focusmm.com/jordan/jo_anamn.htm

Foreign Ministry, The Hashemite Kingdom of Jordan: Jordan First. www.mfa.gov.jo/pages.php?menu_id=374

Jordan Times, The (English language newspaper). www.jordantimes.com/thu/index.htm

Nation by Nation: Population—Jordan. www.nationbynation.com/Jordan/Population.html

World Atlas: Jordan—History, Geography, and Economic Information. www.world-atlas.net/Jordan

World Factbook, The (U.S. CIA). www.cia.gov/cia/publications/factbook/index.html

INDEX